THE BOOK
OF THE
JEWISH YEAR

STEPHEN M. WYLEN

UAHC PRESS
NEW YORK, NEW YORK

To my children:
Jeremy, Elisheva, Shoshana, Golda
May your years be blessed with Jewish ceremony and celebration

Library of Congress Cataloging-in-Publication Data

Wylen, Stephen M., 1952-
The book of the Jewish year / Stephen M. Wylen.
p.   cm.
Includes bibliographical references and index.
Summary: An introduction to the Jewish calendar and the Jewish holiday cycle with the
rituals, foods, symbols, stories, and legends associated with each holiday as well as Hebrew
and English blessings.
ISBN 0-8074-0537-X
1. Fasts and feasts—Judaism—Juvenile literature.
2. Calendar, Jewish—Juvenile literature.
[1. Fasts and feasts—Judaism.]
I. Title.
BM690.W95 1995
296.4'3—dc20   95-36540
                                                                                          CIP
                                                                                           AC

This book is printed on acid-free paper
Copyright © 1996 by the UAHC Press
Book design by Itzhack Shelomi
Manufactured in the United States of America
10 9 8 7 6 5 4 3 2 1

FELDMAN LIBRARY

The Feldman Library Fund was created in 1974 through a gift from the Milton and Sally Feldman Foundation. The Feldman Library Fund which provides for the publication by the UAHC of selected outstanding Jewish books and texts memorializes Sally Feldman who in her lifetime devoted herself to Jewish youth and Jewish learning. Herself an orphan and brought up in an orphanage, she dedicated her efforts to helping Jewish young people get the educational opportunities she had not enjoyed.

In loving memory of my beloved wife Sally
"She was my life, and she is gone;
She was my riches, and I am a pauper."

"Many daughters have done valiantly, but thou excellest them all."

MILTON E. FELDMAN

PICTURE CREDITS

CONTENTS

ACKNOWLEDGMENTS

I am grateful to the many people who helped bring this book to fruition: Rabbi Howard I. Bogot, my longtime teacher; my wife, Cheryl, who supported and encouraged me; my children, who let me try out the drafts of the chapters of this book on them; the teachers and students of Temple Hesed religious school, who tested this book in the classroom; my friend Emily Trunzo, an inspiring teacher and a great Jew; Philip Miller, librarian at the Hebrew Union College-Jewish Institute of Religion, New York campus, who patiently answered my questions and helped me locate resources; and Rabbi Joseph Glazer, of blessed memory, who encouraged me with his avid interest in the project.

In addition, I wish to thank those people at the Union of American Hebrew Congregations Department of Education and on the Commission on Reform Jewish Education who played an important role in shaping the vision and content of this textbook: Rabbi Ellen Greenspan, consulting editor; Rabbi Ellen Nemhauser, managing editor; Judith Goldman, assistant editor and photo editor; Kathy Parnass, copy editor; Stuart Benick, production manager; and Seymour Rossel, publisher. Special thanks to Rabbi Bernard M. Zlotowitz and Rabbi Sharon Forman for carefully reviewing the manuscript and offering invaluable suggestions. My heartfelt gratitude goes to my editor, David Kasakove, for his clear vision and sound advice throughout the many revisions of this book.

Thanks, too, to the following people, who read selected chapters of the manuscript and offered comments: Robin L. Eisenberg, Michael K. Fefferman, Gail Teicher Fellus, Karen L. Goodis, Mimi Krystel, Rabbi Kerry Olitzky, Constance R. Reiter, Roslyn Roucher, Lenore Sandel, Esther Saritzky, Judy Seiff, and Rabbi Jonathan Stein.

My thanks also to those who shared their personal reminiscences for the Jewish Family Album: Rabbi Joan Glazer Farber, Judith Goldman, Rabbi Ellen Greenspan, Rabbi Beth H. Klafter, Sharon Morton, Connie R. Reiter, Sandy Schlanger, Dr. Ira Schweitzer, and Karen Wierzba.

Lastly, I wish to thank those who gave permission to include passages from the following texts: the Central Conference of American Rabbis for *Seder Tu Bishevat: The Festival of Trees* by Adam Fisher and *A Passover Haggadah* edited by Rabbi Herbert Bronstein; The Jewish Museum, Prague, Czech Republic, for the Pavel Friedmann poem from *…I never saw another butterfly…*; and Doubleday, a division of Bantam Doubleday Dell Publishing Group, Inc., for *Anne Frank: The Diary of a Young Girl*.

CHAPTER ONE

JEWISH CALENDAR

To every thing there is a season, and a time to every purpose under heaven.

ECCLESIASTES 3:1

The Jewish Calendar unites the Jewish people. We use the calendar to keep track of the seasons and holy days of the year. As we connect with the cycles of the sun, moon, and stars, the Jewish calendar helps us celebrate the special times in our lives.

1

Honi and the Seasons

A righteous man named Honi lived in the Land of Israel during the days of the ancient Temple. In one particular year, no rain had fallen, although most of the winter rainy season had passed. The people were afraid that their crops would dry out and that spring would never come.

The people asked Honi to pray for rain. Honi prayed, but no rain fell. Then Honi drew a circle and stood inside it.

Honi looked up at the sky and declared: "O God, I pray to You with all my heart and soul. Please give us rain in its proper season. Until the rains come and the circle of the seasons starts again, I vow to stay inside this circle."

Everyone looked up. The sky turned dark and rain began to fall, drop by drop.

But the people were not happy. They turned to Honi and complained: "This rain is too little. It is not enough to water our crops. It seems that this rain is coming down only to release you from your vow to stay inside the circle."

Honi exclaimed to God: "I didn't pray for this little drizzle but for a pouring rain that will fill our wells, ditches, and caves."

Suddenly giant drops of rain began to pour down from the sky. The people turned to Honi and screamed: "These raindrops are too large! If you don't do something, the world will be destroyed!"

Again Honi spoke to God: "It is not for this that I prayed but for rains of blessing that will let us celebrate the seasons and the harvest."

Suddenly the raindrops became smaller. At first, the people were happy. But the rain did not stop! The people ran up to the Temple Mount, which stood above the flooding waters. Once more the people called out to Honi for help.

Again Honi addressed God: "Almighty,

Your rain brings too much blessing. Already there is too much water for our crops. We will not be able to celebrate the harvest spring festival if the water keeps rising. May it be Your will that the rain stop so that we may harvest what You have brought forth from the earth."

At once a wind blew the dark clouds away and the sun began to shine. The people went out to their fields to tend their crops.

Honi looked up at the sky and declared: "God, thank You for the mercy You have shown Your people by letting the circle of the seasons turn once again. And now we shall do our part by celebrating Your seasons and holy days. The time of rejoicing is here."

At last Honi stepped outside the circle. The cycle of the seasons had begun anew.

MITZVOT AND MINHAGIM

Each Jewish holiday has special *mitzvot* and *minhagim* that bring us close to God and teach us the holiday's message. A *mitzvah* מִצְוָה is a commandment from God that is based on the teachings in the Torah. For example, it is a *mitzvah* to rest on Shabbat. A *minhag* מִנְהָג is a custom. It is the way in which people do things. For example, it is a *minhag* to use braided loaves of bread (*challot*) for Shabbat. In this book we will learn about *mitzvot* and *minhagim* for every type of holy day.

IT IS A *MITZVAH* TO
- Celebrate Jewish holidays according to the Jewish calendar.
- Begin the celebration of Jewish holidays at sundown, the beginning of the Jewish day.
- Announce Rosh Chodesh, the beginning of the Jewish month, by saying a special prayer during services on the Shabbat before each new month begins.
- Perform acts of *tzedakah*, righteousness, before each holiday begins.

IT IS A *MINHAG* TO
- Keep a Jewish calendar to help us follow the Jewish holidays.
- Share Jewish holiday traditions with family and friends.

Holidays in the Torah

The calendar of the Jewish holidays is very ancient. When Moses led the Israelites through the Sinai Desert, God instructed Moses to teach the people about six key holidays: Shabbat, Pesach, Shavuot, Rosh Hashanah, Yom Kippur, and Sukot. Since the days of the Bible, other holidays have been added to the Jewish calendar.

The text below is adapted from Chapter 23 of Leviticus, one of the Five Books of the Torah.

Adonai spoke to Moses, saying: Speak to the Israelite people and say to them: These are My fixed times, which you shall proclaim as sacred occasions.

Shabbat

On six days, work may be done, but on the seventh day there shall be a Sabbath of complete rest, a sacred occasion throughout your settlements.

Pesach

On the fourteenth day of the first month, at twilight, there shall be a passover offering to *Adonai*. The fifteenth day of that month is *Adonai*'s Feast of Unleavened Bread. You shall eat unleavened bread for seven days. The first day shall be for you a sacred occasion. You shall not work at your occupations. Seven days you shall make offerings by fire to *Adonai*. The seventh day shall be a sacred occasion. You shall not work at your occupations.

Shavuot

You shall count off seven complete weeks. You must count until the day after the seventh week—fifty days. Then you shall bring an offering of new grain to *Adonai*.... On that same day you shall hold a celebration. It shall be a sacred occasion for you. You shall not work at your occupations.

This is a law for all time in all your settlements throughout the ages.

Rosh Hashanah

On the first day of the seventh month, you shall observe complete rest, a sacred occasion celebrated with loud blasts. You shall not work at your occupations, and you shall bring an offering by fire to *Adonai*.

Yom Kippur

Mark the tenth day of the seventh month as the Day of Atonement. It shall be a sacred occasion for you. You shall practice self-denial, and you shall bring an offering by fire to *Adonai*. You shall do no work throughout that day…. For it is a Day of Atonement, on which you atone before *Adonai* your God….

Sukot

On the fifteenth day of the seventh month, there shall be a Feast of Booths to *Adonai* for seven days…. On the first day you shall take the product of *hadar* trees, branches of palm trees, boughs of leafy trees, and willows of the brook, and you shall rejoice before *Adonai* your God for seven days…. You shall live in booths for seven days in order that future generations may know that I made the Israelite people live in booths when I brought them out of the land of Egypt, I *Adonai* your God.

So Moses declared to the Israelites the set times of *Adonai*.

Many of the Jewish holidays originate in the Torah.

Different Kinds of Days

Lighting candles on Chanukah, the Festival of Lights.

The Jewish calendar tells us which days are *yemei chol* יְמֵי חוֹל—"ordinary days"—and which days are *yemei kodesh* יְמֵי קֹדֶשׁ—"holy days." On a *yom chol* יוֹם חוֹל, an "ordinary day," we do all our usual activities, such as going to school, playing an instrument, or shopping for food. On a *yom kodesh* יוֹם קֹדֶשׁ,

however, we observe certain ceremonies that make the day special. On these days we turn to God and do things that put us in touch with what is special and good.

There are different types of *moadim* מוֹעֲדִים, holidays, in the Jewish calendar:

- *Shalosh Regalim* שָׁלוֹשׁ רְגָלִים—the "Three Pilgrimage Festivals." These are the festivals of Pesach, Shavuot, and Sukot on which Jews in ancient Israel made a pilgrimage—a holy journey—to Jerusalem. These holidays are also called *chagim* חַגִּים (singular, *chag* חַג)—"festivals."

- *Minor Festivals,* of which Chanukah and Purim are the most important. These holidays, also called *chagim*, are different from the *Shalosh Regalim* in two ways. First, they are not mentioned in the Five Books of Moses. Second, they are not days of rest. One may work on a minor festival. Aside from these two differences, a minor festival is still an important holiday.

- *Tzom* צוֹם— a "fast" day or a day of sorrow. The most important fast days are Yom Kippur and Tishah Be'av. Some people also fast on Yom Hashoah— Holocaust Memorial Day. Special fast days are sometimes declared in times of great emergency, during which people pray to God to save them.

- *Yamim Noraim* יָמִים נוֹרָאִים—"Days of Awe." In English we call these days the High Holy Days. They consist of the ten days that start with Rosh Hashanah, the New Year, and end with Yom Kippur, the Day of Atonement. The *Yamim Noraim* is the holiest period of the Jewish year.

Celebrating Rosh Chodesh

The Jewish months are lunar. Each month begins with the new moon, when the moon is just a sliver in the sky. The first day of each month is called Rosh Chodesh רֹאשׁ חֹדֶשׁ—the "Head of the Month." Each month is twenty-nine or thirty days long. During months consisting of thirty days, Rosh Chodesh is celebrated for two days: on the thirtieth day of the old month and on the first day of the new one.

On the Shabbat before Rosh Chodesh, synagogues announce the coming of the new month with a special prayer. We ask God to bless us with health, wealth, and peace during the new month.

In biblical times, Rosh Chodesh was a major festival, observed with special sacrifices, rejoicing, and communal worship. Today Rosh Chodesh is like any other day, except for some additions to the daily prayers.

Over the years, Rosh Chodesh became known as a woman's holiday. Women would not do their usual work on Rosh Chodesh. This mini-vacation for women was seen as a "reward" because, according to one source, the Israelite women at Sinai had refused to contribute their jewelry to the making of the golden calf. Today women in many communities are rediscovering Rosh Chodesh as a time for study, prayer, and celebration.

An earthenware bowl created by potter Lia Lynn Rosen in celebration of Rosh Chodesh.

Why Do We Have Calendars?

A calendar is an agreement among a group of people about what day it is. Most calendars are organized according to our records of the movement of the sun, moon, and stars and the important changes in nature that we see in the world around us. Calendars help us keep track of the seasons of the year. They also help us divide our time among the different things we like to do or have to do—school, work, play, concerts, rest, prayer, and other activities.

The main calendar of the modern world is based on the Julian calendar started by Julius Caesar over 2,000 years ago. (The month of July is named after him.) In 1582, Pope Gregory adapted the Julian calendar to create the Gregorian calendar. This calendar counts the years starting from the birth of Jesus. It is based on the solar year, which measures the time it takes for the earth to circle the sun. The calendar has 365 days divided into twelve months, with a leap year—an extra day—added every four years.

The Jewish Calendar

Many religions, including Judaism, use calendars other than the Gregorian calendar. We have our own special calendar that tells us when to celebrate Shabbat and the holidays. Judaism is older than Christianity and the Gregorian calendar.

The Jewish calendar has twelve lunar months. It also has a leap year. Sometimes we add a thirteenth month to the year. This keeps the Jewish calendar even with the solar year.

The Jewish day begins at sundown. As soon as we can see three stars in the sky, it is the next day.

The days are organized into weeks of seven days. A week is not a portion of a month or a year. According to Jewish tradition, the only purpose of the week is to tell which day is Shabbat, the day of rest. The Gregorian calendar takes its seven-day week from the Jewish calendar. The idea of the week is one of the greatest teachings that Judaism has given the world.

According to Jewish tradition, we know what year it is by counting the number of years from the creation of the world in

JEWISH HOLIDAY CALENDAR

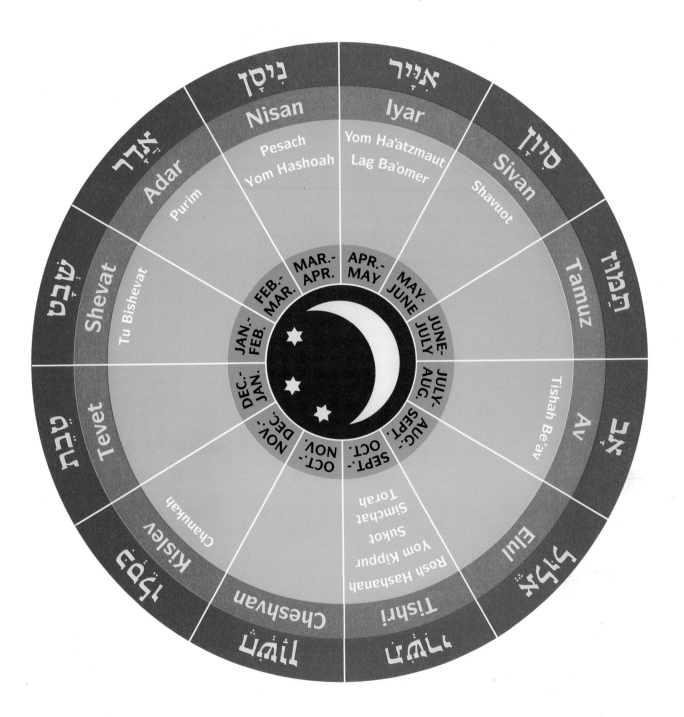

the Torah. In the Jewish calendar the Gregorian year 2000 will correspond to the year 5760 since the creation of the universe.

The names of the Jewish months come from the ancient Babylonians, who were great astronomers. The months are:

NISAN, IYAR, SIVAN (SPRING)
TAMUZ, AV, ELUL (SUMMER)
TISHRI, CHESHVAN, KISLEV (FALL)
TEVET, SHEVAT, ADAR (WINTER)

In leap years there is an extra month of Adar, Adar II (Second Adar).

Many Jews have special calendars called Jewish-Gregorian calendars. A Jewish-Gregorian calendar gives both the Gregorian and the Jewish date for each day. It provides us with Jewish information, such as the time Shabbat begins each week, the dates of Jewish holidays, and what portions to read from the Torah on Shabbat and holidays. It also gives us the dates of civil holidays, as well as those of the Christian holidays, like Christmas and Easter, that our neighbors may celebrate.

SUMMARY

Calendars are important because they help us keep track of the seasons of the year and of the things we do in each season. The Jewish calendar is a lunar calendar that follows the cycles of the moon. Although we live according to many different calendars and schedules, the Jewish calendar is an important part of what makes us special. In this book we will look at all the festivals and holy days of the Jewish year and discover ways in which they can enrich our lives.

CHAPTER TWO

SHABBAT

More than Israel has kept the Sabbath, the Sabbath has kept Israel.

AHAD HA-AM

Shabbat
שַׁבָּת
is the seventh day of the week, the day of rest. On Shabbat we remember that God created the world and then rested. We remember that we were slaves and God made us free. We enjoy Shabbat as a day of rest, holiness, and joy.

The Two Angels

Each Friday evening God sends two angels, a good angel and a bad angel, to visit every Jewish home.

When the angels enter one home, they see the Shabbat candles shining bright. At the Shabbat dinner table the family members sing together the *Kiddush* blessing. The good angel prays, "May the next Shabbat be just like this one." The bad angel is forced to answer "Amen."

When the two angels enter another home, they see that the Shabbat candles are not lit. Nothing is ready for Shabbat. The family members are arguing and screaming at one another. The bad angel prays, "May the next Shabbat be just like this one." The good angel is forced to answer "Amen."

MITZVOT AND MINHAGIM

IT IS A *MITZVAH* TO
- Observe Shabbat from sundown on Friday until sundown on Saturday.
- Welcome Shabbat with a fine meal in the company of family and friends.
- Welcome Shabbat by reciting a blessing over Shabbat candles, *Kiddush* over wine or grape juice, and blessings before and after the Shabbat meal.
- Celebrate Shabbat with activities that lead to joy, rest, and holiness, including time devoted to Jewish learning.
- Do no work on Shabbat.
- Worship with a congregation of Jews on Shabbat in a synagogue or another gathering place.
- Conclude Shabbat with the ceremony of *Havdalah*.

IT IS A *MINHAG* TO
- Eat a braided loaf of bread called challah.
- Enjoy Shabbat by singing Shabbat songs called *zemirot* זְמִרוֹת, especially at the dinner table.

Shabbat in the Torah

The very first story in the Torah introduces us to Shabbat. It tells us about the first Shabbat after God finished creating the universe.

The heaven and the earth were finished, and all that was in them. On the seventh day God finished the work that God had been doing, and God ceased on the seventh day from all the work that God had done. And God blessed the seventh day and made it holy, because on that day God finished all the work of creation that God had done.

GENESIS 2:1-3

The Ten Commandments are the basic rules for society. The Fourth Commandment concerns Shabbat observance. Shabbat rest is a great gift that Judaism has given to all the nations of the world. In the Book of Exodus, the Torah says:

Remember זָכוֹר the Shabbat and keep it holy. Six days you shall labor and do all your work, but the seventh day is a Shabbat of *Adonai* your God: You shall not do any work—you, your son or daughter, your male or female slave, or your cattle, or the stranger who is within your settlements. For in six days *Adonai* made heaven and earth and sea, and all that is in them, and God rested on the seventh day; therefore, *Adonai* blessed the Shabbat and made it holy.

EXODUS 20: 8-11

The Torah repeats the Ten Commandments in the Book of Deuteronomy:

Observe שָׁמוֹר the Shabbat and keep it holy, as *Adonai* your God has commanded you....Remember that you were a slave in the land of Egypt and that *Adonai* your God freed you from there with a mighty hand and an outstretched arm; therefore, *Adonai* your God has commanded you to observe the Shabbat.

DEUTERONOMY 5:12-15

Notice that the two versions of the Ten Commandments begin with a different word. One says *Zachor* זָכוֹר, "Remember." The other says *Shamor* שָׁמוֹר, "Observe." What is the difference between *Shamor* and *Zachor*?

Here are some of the answers:
- *Shamor* means to be careful to observe the laws of Shabbat. *Zachor* means to welcome Shabbat with food, wine, and joyfulness.
- God said both words at once and the Jews heard them both at once.
- *Shamor* is for the Jewish people, who are commanded by God to observe Shabbat. *Zachor* is for the other nations. Even though people of other nations are not commanded to observe Shabbat, every nation in the world has adopted the idea of a day of rest.

This painting by contemporary artist Sara Novenson depicts Lechah Dodi, *a well-known song that is sung on Friday evening to welcome Shabbat.*

Preparing the House for Shabbat

Friday afternoon is a special time for performing acts of tzedakah in Jewish communities. The poor can then use the money to buy what they need to celebrate Shabbat.

We get ready for Shabbat by taking time during the week to prepare our home for Friday evening. We should finish our cooking, cleaning, laundry, and lawn work before Shabbat begins so that we can focus our attention on celebrating Shabbat. In Israel most people get off from work early on Friday so that they have time to prepare for Shabbat. In other countries people may have to prepare for Shabbat on Thursday evening.

Blessings at the Shabbat Table

We welcome Shabbat by reciting the blessing over the candles and *Kiddush* קִדּוּשׁ, the blessing over the wine or grape juice. Before the meal we recite the blessing over *challot*, which is called *Hamotzi* הַמּוֹצִיא. After Shabbat dinner we recite *Birkat Hamazon* בִּרְכַּת הַמָּזוֹן, the blessing after meals.

Most often two candles are placed on the table. In some homes a candle is also lit for each child in the family. After lighting the candles, some Jews encircle the flames with their hands three times, as if to bring Shabbat closer. Then they cover their eyes and recite the following blessing:

בָּרוּךְ אַתָּה, יְיָ אֱלֹהֵינוּ, מֶלֶךְ הָעוֹלָם, אֲשֶׁר קִדְּשָׁנוּ בְּמִצְוֹתָיו וְצִוָּנוּ לְהַדְלִיק נֵר שֶׁל שַׁבָּת.

Blessed are You, Adonai our God, Ruler of the universe, who makes us holy with mitzvot and commands us to kindle the lights of Shabbat.

Unlike other times when we recite a blessing before we perform a *mitzvah*, we say or sing this blessing after we have lit the candles. We do this in order to light the flames before Shabbat begins.

זֵכֶר לִיצִיאַת מִצְרָיִם. כִּי־בָנוּ בָחַרְתָּ
וְאוֹתָנוּ קִדַּשְׁתָּ מִכָּל־הָעַמִּים, וְשַׁבַּת
קָדְשְׁךָ בְּאַהֲבָה וּבְרָצוֹן הִנְחַלְתָּנוּ.
בָּרוּךְ אַתָּה יְיָ, מְקַדֵּשׁ הַשַּׁבָּת.

*Blessed are You, Adonai our God, Ruler of
the universe, who makes us holy with mitzvot
and takes delight in us. In love and favor God
has made the holy Shabbat our heritage as a
reminder of the work of creation. This day is
first among our sacred days, a remembrance of
the Exodus from Egypt. O God, You have
chosen us and set us apart from all the peoples
and in love and favor have given us the
Shabbat as a sacred inheritance. Blessed are
You, Adonai our God, for the Shabbat and its
holiness.*

We then lift up the *Kiddush* cup to
recite the blessing over the wine or grape
juice. The *Kiddush* cup is usually a
decorative cup that is used especially for
Kiddush. There are two blessings. First, we
say the blessing over the wine or grape
juice. Then, we say a longer blessing to
welcome Shabbat. We use wine or grape
juice to welcome Shabbat because the
fruit of the vine is a symbol of joy. We
say:

בָּרוּךְ אַתָּה, יְיָ אֱלֹהֵינוּ, מֶלֶךְ הָעוֹלָם,
בּוֹרֵא פְּרִי הַגָּפֶן.

*Blessed are You, Adonai our God, Ruler of
the universe, Creator of the fruit of the vine.*

בָּרוּךְ אַתָּה, יְיָ אֱלֹהֵינוּ, מֶלֶךְ הָעוֹלָם,
אֲשֶׁר קִדְּשָׁנוּ בְּמִצְוֹתָיו וְרָצָה בָנוּ,
וְשַׁבַּת קָדְשׁוֹ בְּאַהֲבָה וּבְרָצוֹן
הִנְחִילָנוּ, זִכָּרוֹן לְמַעֲשֵׂה בְרֵאשִׁית.
כִּי הוּא יוֹם תְּחִלָּה לְמִקְרָאֵי קֹדֶשׁ,

Before we begin the Shabbat meal, we
lift up the challah חַלָּה, the special
Shabbat bread. In many Jewish homes
two challah loaves are served on Shabbat.
These two loaves represent the double
portion of manna that the Israelites
received from God before each Sabbath.
We then recite:

בָּרוּךְ אַתָּה, יְיָ אֱלֹהֵינוּ, מֶלֶךְ הָעוֹלָם,
הַמּוֹצִיא לֶחֶם מִן הָאָרֶץ.

*Blessed are You, Adonai our God, Ruler of
the universe, for causing bread to come forth
from the earth.*

Everyone then eats a piece of challah
and begins the meal.

Havdalah

Havdalah הַבְדָּלָה is the ceremony that marks the end of Shabbat on Saturday night. Shabbat officially ends when three stars appear in the sky. To make *Havdalah*, we need three things: a *Kiddush* cup with wine or juice, a spice box, and a candle with at least two wicks.

Havdalah means "Separating one thing from another." To tell things apart, we use our five senses. We use our five senses to identify what is Shabbat and what is *chol*, an ordinary day. We use our cup, our spices, and our candle to enjoy all five senses.

At dusk on Saturday, after three stars have appeared in the sky, we take part in the Havdalah *service, which marks the end of Shabbat and the beginning of a new week.*

We begin the *Havdalah* ceremony by reciting some biblical verses that remind us of God's salvation and how God saves us in times of trouble. Then we recite the *Havdalah* blessings.

First, we pick up the *Kiddush* cup and recite the blessing over the wine or juice. Then, we pick up the spice box. If it has bells on it, we shake it to hear them ring. Before we smell the sweet spices we say:

בָּרוּךְ אַתָּה, יְיָ אֱלֹהֵינוּ, מֶלֶךְ הָעוֹלָם, בּוֹרֵא מִינֵי בְשָׂמִים.

Blessed are You, Adonai our God, Ruler of the universe, Creator of all spices.

We pass around the spice box for everyone to smell. At this point, we hold up our hands to the candle to feel its warmth. We use the light by curling our fingers with the palms up and looking at the candlelight reflecting in our fingernails so that we can see the difference between light and dark. We say:

בָּרוּךְ אַתָּה, יְיָ אֱלֹהֵינוּ, מֶלֶךְ הָעוֹלָם, בּוֹרֵא מְאוֹרֵי הָאֵשׁ.

Blessed are You, Adonai our God, Ruler of the universe, Creator of the light of fire.

We say the special *Havdalah* blessing about separating one thing from another:

בָּרוּךְ אַתָּה, יְיָ אֱלֹהֵינוּ, מֶלֶךְ הָעוֹלָם, הַמַּבְדִּיל בֵּין קֹדֶשׁ לְחוֹל, בֵּין אוֹר לְחֹשֶׁךְ, בֵּין יוֹם הַשְּׁבִיעִי לְשֵׁשֶׁת יְמֵי הַמַּעֲשֶׂה. בָּרוּךְ אַתָּה יְיָ, הַמַּבְדִּיל בֵּין קֹדֶשׁ לְחוֹל.

Blessed are You, Adonai our God, Ruler of the universe, who separates the holy from the commonplace, light from darkness, the seventh day of rest from the six days of labor. Blessed are You, Adonai our God, who separates the holy from the commonplace.

To conclude the service, the leader takes a sip of wine and dips the candle into the wine to put out the flame. We listen to the sizzling sound. We then sing *Eliyahu Hanavi* אֵלִיָּהוּ הַנָּבִיא, "Elijah the Prophet." We sing this song because we long for Elijah the Prophet to arrive at the end of Shabbat and tell us that the perfect time, the Messianic Age, has come. Then this Shabbat would never have to end! At the conclusion of the ceremony, we all say *Shavua Tov* שָׁבוּעַ טוֹב, "Good Week," to one another.

JEWISH FAMILY ALBUM

When I was a rabbinic student in Los Angeles, one of my professors would invite students for Shabbat dinner. At his house on one Friday night, I saw for the first time a parent bless his children. I was so inspired by this Shabbat ritual that I promised myself that when I had children, I would bless them every Shabbat.

Now I have a two-and-a-half-year-old daughter. An important part of our Friday night ritual is the blessing I give her after I light the candles. I put my arms around Adina and say the following blessing:

יְבָרֶכְךָ יְיָ וְיִשְׁמְרֶךָ.
יָאֵר יְיָ פָּנָיו אֵלֶיךָ וִיחֻנֶּךָּ.
יִשָּׂא יְיָ פָּנָיו אֵלֶיךָ וְיָשֵׂם לְךָ שָׁלוֹם.

May God bless you and guard you. May the light of God shine upon you, and may God be gracious to you. May the presence of God be with you and give you peace.

I hope to make the blessing more personal when she is a little older and better able to understand. I hope that when Adina has grown, she will remember the blessings she received on Shabbat and will continue our family ritual.

RABBI ELLEN GREENSPAN

What Is Work?

The Torah says: "Six days you shall labor and do all your work, but the seventh day is a Shabbat of *Adonai* your God. You shall not do any work." We may not work on Shabbat. But what is "work"?

In biblical times, the Jewish leader Ezra the Scribe was unhappy because the Jews of Jerusalem were using Shabbat as a shopping day. Ezra locked the city gates to keep the people away from the shops. Ezra regarded buying and selling things as work. Ezra thought that even *talking* about business was work. Thus no business or shopping on Shabbat became the Jewish law.

In the *Mishnah*, the central book of Jewish law that was completed almost 1,800 years ago, the rabbis listed thirty-nine activities that are forbidden on Shabbat. These include planting, plowing, reaping, baking, sewing, writing, building, putting out a fire, lighting a fire, and moving things from one property to another.

The above list has nothing to do with how difficult a task is. You can move around all the furniture in your house on Shabbat, but you cannot move a chair from inside the house to the outside. According to the rabbis, the list included all the types of work that the Israelites took part in when they built the Tabernacle in the Sinai Desert.

Some people believe that all the changes that have occurred since that ancient time have made the thirty-nine activities listed in the *Mishnah* outdated. But others think we should still observe or add to the laws written in the *Mishnah*. For example, some Jews won't drive a car on Shabbat because running the engine can be compared to lighting a fire. Other Jews, however, do drive on Shabbat. Some activities are obviously not in the spirit of Shabbat. Each individual needs to study Jewish texts and choose a level of Shabbat observance that is meaningful for him or her.

The Spirit of Shabbat: Rest, Holiness, and Joy

What we do with our time on Shabbat is just as important as not working on this special day. Everything we do on Shabbat should be for the purpose of one of these three things: *menuchah* מְנוּחָה, "rest"; *kedushah* קְדוּשָׁה, "holiness"; and *oneg* עֹנֶג, "joy."

Shabbat *menuchah* is a special kind of rest. When we work, we rest occasionally to regain our strength so we can work harder. On Shabbat we do not rest in order to work but to enjoy resting. We might enjoy taking a nap on Shabbat afternoon or a pleasant walk in a park. We might enjoy getting together with our family or with a few friends.

Kedushah, the holiness of Shabbat, begins when we welcome Shabbat with blessings. We worship God when we attend synagogue services on Friday evening and Saturday morning. Many congregations hold services after dinner on Friday. These services include songs, prayers, and a sermon. In other congregations Shabbat services begin just before sundown each Friday evening. The service is very brief and includes beautiful music. Everyone is finished praying in time to go home for the Shabbat meal.

Saturday morning services include readings from the Torah and the *haftarah* הַפְטָרָה portions and prayers and songs of praise to God. Many young men and

A *HAFTARAH* PORTION IS A READING FROM THE BIBLICAL BOOKS OF THE PROPHETS THAT FOLLOWS THE READING OF THE TORAH ON SHABBAT AND HOLIDAYS. WHEN THE SAGES SELECTED *HAFTARAH* PORTIONS FROM THE PROPHETS, THEY CHOSE READINGS THAT CONTAIN A REFERENCE TO AN EVENT OR THEME IN THE TORAH PORTION READ BEFORE IT.

Each Saturday morning benai mitzvah *and other congregation members read from the Torah.*

women become a bar or bat mitzvah at this service. In addition to attending services, many congregants meet to study and discuss the weekly Torah portion.

We enjoy Shabbat *oneg* by eating a special Shabbat dinner. Until recent times, most people in the world ate only two meals a day, but Jews often ate a third meal on Shabbat afternoon. Eating and drinking give us joy. Having guests or visiting with friends is also part of Shabbat *oneg*. The custom of having refreshments after services and talking with our friends in the synagogue is called *Oneg Shabbat,* the "Joy of Shabbat." Shabbat is a time for rest, holiness, and joy.

Rabbi Isaac Mayer Wise, the founder of Reform Judaism in America, introduced the late Friday evening service. Until that time, Friday services had taken place before dinner, and the main Shabbat service had always been held on Saturday morning.

TIMES AND PLACES

Kabbalat Shabbat in Sixteenth-Century Safed

Around the year 1530, many great rabbis gathered in the town of Safed, located in the Galilee mountain region of the Land of Israel.

The rabbis of Safed had a special custom for welcoming Shabbat called *Kabbalat Shabbat* קַבָּלַת שַׁבָּת.

On Friday afternoon they would bathe and dress all in white. Then they would gather at the edge of town. As the sun sank in the west, the rabbis sang psalms and songs while they marched to their synagogues. The rabbis thought of Shabbat as a beautiful bride and the Jewish people as her husband. They regarded Shabbat worship as the wedding ceremony. The rabbis accompanied the bride on a wedding march through the town to their synagogues.

One of the rabbis of Safed, Rabbi Solomon Alkabetz, wrote a song called *Lechah Dodi* לְכָה דוֹדִי to welcome the Sabbath bride. Today Jews all over the world sing this song on Friday night.

At many Jewish summer camps the campers dress in white on Friday night and sing Jewish songs as they walk from their cabins to the Friday evening service. They are following the *minhag* of the holy rabbis of Safed.

Campers and counselors celebrate Kabbalat Shabbat *at a Jewish summer camp.*

SUMMARY

Shabbat is the seventh day of the week, the day of rest. Some people consider Shabbat to be the most special of all Jewish holidays because it comes every week. Shabbat provides us with a needed break from our everyday lives. It can be compared to taking a deep breath and relaxing. The spirit of Shabbat can be summed up in three words: rest, holiness, and joy. Everything we do on Shabbat should fall into one of these three categories.

In the next chapter we will begin to study the High Holy Days, the most important of the Jewish holidays that come just once a year.

CHAPTER THREE

ROSH HASHANAH

A cobbler passed by the window of Rabbi Levi Yitzhak and called out, "Have you nothing to mend?" The rabbi began to cry, "Woe is me! Rosh Hashanah is almost here, and I have not yet mended myself!"

ZICHRON LA-RISHONIM

Rosh Hashanah רֹאשׁ הַשָּׁנָה is the beginning of the Jewish year. It falls on the first of Tishri, in the early fall. Rosh Hashanah celebrates the birthday of the world. On this day we praise God as Creator of the universe. Rosh Hashanah begins the *Yamim Noraim*, the ten "Days of Awe," when we weigh our actions of the past year and promise to do better in the year to come.

The Book of Days

On Rosh Hashanah, Reb Yakov sat in the synagogue. As he listened to the cantor chant, he closed his eyes and began to daydream:

The Holy One sat upon the Throne of Judgment, surrounded by angels. Reb Yakov saw himself in the dream. He stood before the Heavenly Court. The angels opened the Book of Life to the page that had Reb Yakov's name inscribed on it. It was filled with all he had done during the past year. Not even the smallest deed had been overlooked. All of Reb Yakov's good deeds were written in black ink on the Credit side of the page. All of his bad deeds were written in red ink on the Debit side of the page. Reb Yakov's many good deeds were balanced against his bad deeds.

In his imagination Reb Yakov watched as the trial took place. All of Reb Yakov's *mitzvot* turned into angels. They rose to speak in his defense. Then Satan, the prosecuting angel, stood up and listed all of Reb Yakov's sins.

Reb Yakov waited for the verdict. He wondered whether he would be inscribed for a year of blessing. He waited and waited. Suddenly the defending angel stood before him.

"Reb Yakov," he said, "the Holy One has not yet rendered a verdict."

"But I don't understand. Why must I wait?"

"Today is the Day of Judgment. On this day three books are opened. One is filled with the names of the completely righteous. Another is filled with the names of the completely wicked."

"Is my name written in either of those books?" asked Reb Yakov.

"No, that is why you must wait," the

angel responded. "For both the completely righteous and the completely wicked, the Holy One renders and seals the verdict at once. But your name, Reb Yakov, has been written into the third book—the book that lists those who are not entirely good nor entirely bad."

"What shall become of me?" Reb Yakov wondered.

"Your verdict has been suspended until Yom Kippur. During the Days of Awe, if you repent, pray, and perform acts of *tzedakah*, then you will be inscribed in the Book of Life."

Suddenly Reb Yakov woke from his daydream. He listened to the cantor chant. As he opened the pages of his prayer book, he promised to return to God in the days ahead.

MITZVOT AND MINHAGIM

IT IS A *MITZVAH* TO

- Observe Rosh Hashanah on the first of Tishri as a festival and a High Holy Day.
- Welcome Rosh Hashanah with blessings over candles and wine and with a festive meal.
- Attend synagogue worship services.
- Not work or go to school on Rosh Hashanah.
- Hear the sound of the *shofar*, the ram's horn. We blow the *shofar* in the synagogue during the morning worship services.
- Repent for all our sins of the past year.
- Give *tzedakah* at this time of year.

IT IS A *MINHAG* TO

- Attend worship services on the Saturday night before Rosh Hashanah to repent for our sins of the past year. This service is called *Selichot* סְלִיחוֹת, "Forgiveness."
- Eat a round challah. The round challah is like a crown for God.
- Express our hopes for a sweet new year by eating apples and honey.
- Send Rosh Hashanah greeting cards to friends and relatives.
- Visit the graves of our ancestors so that the memory of their lives will inspire us in the coming year.
- Observe the custom of *Tashlich* on the afternoon of Rosh Hashanah.

Unetaneh Tokef

One of the most important Rosh Hashanah prayers is *Unetaneh Tokef* וּנְתַנֶּה תֹּקֶף. This prayer sums up the meaning of the High Holy Days. Here is a shortened version:

Let us proclaim the sacred power of this day;

It is awesome and full of dread.

For on this day Your reign is exalted,

The daily Jewish prayer book is called a siddur סִדּוּר. *We have a separate prayer book for the Days of Awe. We call this book a* machzor מַחְזוֹר, *which is the Hebrew word for cycle.*

Your throne is established in everlasting love….

You open the book of our days, and what is written there speaks for itself, for it is signed by every person….

As the shepherd seeks out his flock, and makes the sheep pass under his staff, so do You count and consider every soul, setting the boundary of every creature's life, and deciding its destiny.

On Rosh Hashanah it is written, on Yom Kippur it is sealed:

How many shall pass on, how many shall come to be;

Who shall live and who shall die….

But repentance תְּשׁוּבָה, prayer תְּפִלָּה, and *tzedakah* צְדָקָה save us from the severe decree.

This is Your glory: You are slow to anger, ready to forgive. *Adonai*, it is not the death of sinners You seek, but that they should turn from their ways and live….

Humanity's origin is dust, and dust is our end.

Each of us is a shattered pot, grass that must wither, a flower that will fade, a shadow moving on, a cloud passing by, a particle of dust floating on the wind, a dream soon forgotten.

But You are the Ruler, the everlasting God!

Apples and Honey

It is a *minhag* to start the new year with something sweet. We place sliced apples and a dish of honey on the dinner table on the eve of Rosh Hashanah. After we light the candles and recite *Kiddush*, each person at the table dips a slice of apple into the honey. We say the following blessing over the fruit:

בָּרוּךְ אַתָּה, יְיָ אֱלֹהֵינוּ, מֶלֶךְ הָעוֹלָם,
בּוֹרֵא פְּרִי הָעֵץ.

Blessed are You, Adonai our God, Ruler of the universe, Creator of the fruit of the tree.

We then say:

יְהִי רָצוֹן מִלְּפָנֶיךָ, יְיָ אֱלֹהֵינוּ וֵאלֹהֵי
אֲבוֹתֵינוּ, שֶׁתְּחַדֵּשׁ עָלֵינוּ שָׁנָה
טוֹבָה וּמְתֻקָה.

May it be Your will, Adonai our God and God of our people, that the new year be good and sweet for us.

We then eat the apples and honey.

Blowing the Shofar

The *shofar* שׁוֹפָר is an animal horn that we blow like a trumpet. It is usually a ram's horn, but a *shofar* can be made from the horn of any kosher animal except a cow. Today the use of a long and beautiful antelope horn is popular. Unlike a trumpet, the *shofar* has no mouthpiece. It is difficult to blow. *Shofar* blowers spend many hours practicing before Rosh Hashanah.

The *shofar* blower should be someone who is admired in the community, a person who is well liked and does good deeds. The *shofar* blower is called the *ba'al tekiah* בַּעַל תְּקִיעָה. Another person stands next to the *ba'al tekiah* and calls out the notes.

There are three kinds of notes. The *tekiah* תְּקִיעָה is a single blast. The *shevarim* שְׁבָרִים is a set of three blasts. The *teruah* תְּרוּעָה is a set of nine very short blasts. During the *shofar* service the *ba'al tekiah* blows these three notes in different combinations as they are called out. At the end of the *shofar* service, a very long *tekiah*, the *tekiah gedolah* תְּקִיעָה גְדוֹלָה, is blown.

When it is time to blow the *shofar*, the whole congregation stands. They recite the blessing for the *mitzvah* of hearing the *shofar*:

בָּרוּךְ אַתָּה, יְיָ אֱלֹהֵינוּ, מֶלֶךְ הָעוֹלָם,
אֲשֶׁר קִדְּשָׁנוּ בְּמִצְוֹתָיו וְצִוָּנוּ לִשְׁמוֹעַ
קוֹל שׁוֹפָר.

*Blessed are You, Adonai our God, Ruler of
the universe, who makes us holy with mitzvot
and calls us to hear the sound of the shofar.*

בָּרוּךְ אַתָּה, יְיָ אֱלֹהֵינוּ, מֶלֶךְ הָעוֹלָם,
שֶׁהֶחֱיָנוּ וְקִיְּמָנוּ וְהִגִּיעָנוּ לַזְּמָן הַזֶּה.

*Blessed are You, Adonai our God, Ruler of
the universe, for giving us life, for sustaining
us, and for enabling us to reach this season.*

There are many reasons why we blow
the *shofar* on Rosh Hashanah.

According to Maimonides, the great
Jewish scholar, we blow the *shofar* on
Rosh Hashanah to say, "Wake up! Wake
up, everyone who is asleep! Remember
God, your Creator! Instead of going
around doing things that are not important or worthwhile, take some time to
think about what you can do to make
yourself into a better person. Give up
doing bad things!"

*Joshua succeeded Moses as the leader of the Jewish people. His bravery and nobility in battle helped
him lead the Israelites to the Promised Land. On God's command, Joshua ordered seven priests to
blow their shofars for seven days while they circled the walls of the city of Jericho. On the seventh
day, as the priests were making their seventh circle around the city, the walls of Jericho crumbled,
enabling the Jewish people to enter the city.*

Rabbi Saadia Gaon gave some reasons for blowing the *shofar*:

- Rosh Hashanah is the birthday of the world. [It is like a birthday party, at which we blow horns.]
- The *shofar* reminds us of the ram that Abraham sacrificed in place of his son Isaac.

- When God gave us the Ten Commandments at Mount Sinai, the Israelites heard the sound of a *shofar*. The *shofar* reminds us that God gives us laws and rules to obey.
- The *shofar* is the call of redemption. The *shofar* reminds us that God redeems the Jewish people.

JEWISH FAMILY ALBUM

There is a custom that on Rosh Hashanah afternoon, Jews go to a stream, lake, or beach and throw bread crumbs into the water as a sign that they are throwing off their sins of the past year. This custom is called *Tashlich* תַּשְׁלִיךְ. As we throw the crumbs, we recite the following passage from the prophet Micah 7:18-20:

> Who is a God like You,
> Forgiving sin
> And sending away evil?
> God will take us back in love;

> You will cover up our wrongs,
> You will hurl all our sins
> Into the deep of the sea.
> You will keep faith with Jacob,
> Loyalty to Abraham,
> As you promised an oath to our ancestors
> In days gone by.

My family observes *Tashlich* in the following way. First, we study Jewish teachings on how to repent. Then, we each take a paper towel and write a confession on it, using a washable-ink pen. We think about what we have written, and when we are feeling truly sorry about what we have confessed, we put the folded paper towel into a big bowl of water. After all the paper towels have turned to mush in the water, we blow the *shofar* to show that God has forgiven us.

RABBI STEPHEN M. WYLEN

Jewish Greetings

This colorful Shanah Tovah *card was made in Germany in the 1920s for the American Jewish public.*

Jews have greetings for every type of special day. On ordinary days the greeting is *Shalom* שָׁלוֹם, "Peace," or *Shalom Alechem* שָׁלוֹם עֲלֵיכֶם, "Peace Be with You." The correct response is *Alechem Hashalom* עֲלֵיכֶם הַשָּׁלוֹם, "With You, Peace." On Shabbat we say *Shabbat Shalom* שַׁבָּת שָׁלוֹם, "Sabbath Peace."

On the Jewish festivals we say in Hebrew *Chag Sameach* חַג שָׂמֵחַ, "Happy Holiday."

A few weeks before Rosh Hashanah, we begin to greet our Jewish friends with *Leshanah Tovah Tikatevu* לְשָׁנָה טוֹבָה תִּכָּתֵבוּ, "May You Be Inscribed [in the Book of Life] for a Good Year." Or we can just say *Leshanah Tovah* לְשָׁנָה טוֹבָה, "To a Good Year."

From the afternoon of Rosh Hashanah until after Yom Kippur, we say *Gemar Chatimah Tovah* גְּמַר חֲתִימָה טוֹבָה, "May You Be Sealed in the Book of Life for Good."

THE SHABBAT BETWEEN ROSH HASHANAH AND YOM KIPPUR IS CALLED SHABBAT SHUVAH שַׁבָּת תְּשׁוּבָה. THIS NAME COMES FROM THE BOOK OF HOSEA: "SHUVAH, YISRAEL ... RETURN, O ISRAEL, TO *ADONAI* YOUR GOD...." (14:2)

SUMMARY

Rosh Hashanah, the Jewish new year, is celebrated on the first of Tishri. Rosh Hashanah is also called *Yom Hadin* יוֹם הַדִּין, the "Day of Judgment," because on this day God judges our good and bad deeds. The sound of the *shofar* calls us to turn to God. During the ten Days of Awe, we should strive to repent, pray, and perform acts of *tzedakah*.

In the next chapter we will reflect more on the topics of repentance and forgiveness as we learn about Yom Kippur.

CHAPTER FOUR

YOM KIPPUR

Happy are you, Israel! Who purifies you, and before whom do you make yourselves pure? You stand before your Maker, the Blessed Holy One, who is full of mercy and desires to forgive you.

AFTER RABBI AKIVA

Yom Kippur

יוֹם כִּפּוּר

is the Day of Atonement. We observe Yom Kippur on the tenth day of the month of Tishri, at the end of the ten Days of Awe. Yom Kippur is a fast day and a day of rest. On this day we atone for all of our sins of the past year and we promise to improve our behavior. We begin the new year feeling renewed.

31

Jonah and the Big Fish

The word of God came to Jonah: "Go to the great city of Ninevah, the capital of the Assyrians. Tell the people to return to me or else I will destroy them for their sins."

Jonah did not want to go to Ninevah. He did not care about the people of Ninevah. He went down to the seacoast and boarded a ship that was leaving for a distant land. God sent such a great storm upon the sea that the ship was in danger of breaking up. All the people on the ship prayed to their own gods, but the storm continued. The ship's crew found Jonah asleep in the hold of the vessel.

"How can you sleep when we are all in danger?" cried the ship's captain. "Up," he said, "and pray to your God. Perhaps your God will save us."

The shipmates said to one another, "Let us cast lots and find out who has brought this terrible storm upon us." They cast lots, and the lot fell on Jonah. They asked him, "Who are you? Where are you from?"

"I am a Hebrew," he replied. "I worship *Adonai*, the God of heaven, who made both the sea and the land. I have fled from God."

"What can we do to make the sea calm?" the men asked.

"Throw me overboard," Jonah answered. "Then the sea will calm down." So they threw Jonah overboard and the sea stopped raging. God sent a huge fish to swallow Jonah. Jonah remained in the belly of the fish for three days and three nights.

He prayed to God to save him. God commanded the fish and it spit Jonah out onto dry land.

Then Jonah went to Ninevah and proclaimed, "In forty days Ninevah shall be destroyed." When the people heard Jonah, they feared God. The king of Assyria ordered everyone in Ninevah to fast and pray to God. When God saw what they did, how they were turning back from their evil ways, God spared the city of Ninevah and did not destroy it.

This made Jonah very angry. He prayed to God: "O God! Why did you send me here if you were only going to spare the people of Ninevah? They don't deserve a second chance!"

Jonah went to sit outside the walls of the city. God provided a gourd plant, which grew up over Jonah to provide shade for his head. Jonah was very happy about the plant.

But the next day the plant died. The sun beat down on Jonah's head, and he felt faint. Jonah begged for death.

Then God said to Jonah: "You care for a plant that you did not work for and did not tend, which appeared overnight and died overnight. Shouldn't I care about Ninevah, that great city full of people who do not yet know their right hand from their left, as well as many beasts?"

ADAPTED FROM THE BOOK OF JONAH

MITZVOT AND MINHAGIM

IT IS A *MITZVAH* TO

- Fast on Yom Kippur. From sundown to sundown, we drink no water and eat no food. Children under the age of thirteen do not have to fast, but they might eat less and avoid snacks.
- Enjoy a festive meal on the eve of Yom Kippur. We are happy before this serious day because we are about to ask forgiveness from God, who loves to forgive.
- Rest from all work.
- Pray with a congregation during the worship services of Yom Kippur.

- Remember parents and ancestors who have died. We light *Yizkor* יִזְכֹּר (memorial) candles on the eve of Yom Kippur. We recite the *Yizkor* service in synagogue on Yom Kippur.

IT IS A *MINHAG* TO

- Do a *mitzvah* as soon as Yom Kippur ends. Many Jews hammer in the first nail of their *sukah* as soon as they get home from services.
- Break the Yom Kippur fast with a joyous meal.

Our Covenant with God

On Yom Kippur we stand before God and promise to follow God's *mitzvot*. In the following text from the Torah, Moses sets forth what God expects of the Jewish people. As Moses addresses the Children of Israel, he explains that they have entered into a covenant—an agreement with God. It is a covenant that shall last for all time.

> Moses summoned all Israel and said to them: You stand this day, all of you, before *Adonai* your God ... to enter into the sworn covenant that *Adonai* your God makes with you this day....

> It is not with you alone that I make this sworn covenant: I make it with those who are standing here with us today before *Adonai* our God, and equally with all who are not here with us today.

> For this commandment, which I command you this day, is not too hard for you, nor too remote. It is not in heaven, that you should say: "Who will go up for us to heaven and bring it down to us, that we may do it?" Nor is it beyond the sea, that you should say: "Who will cross the sea for us and bring it over to us, that we may do it?" No, it is very near to you, in your mouth and in your heart, and you can do it.

The Torah is an expression of the eternal covenant between God and the Jewish people.

See, I have set before you this day life and good, death and evil. For I command you this day to love *Adonai*, to walk in God's ways and to keep the commandments, laws, and teachings of your God....

I call heaven and earth to witness against you this day. I have set before you life and death, blessing and curse. Choose life ... by loving *Adonai* your God, listening to God's voice, and holding fast to God's ways. Then you shall endure in the land that *Adonai* promised to your ancestors, to Abraham, Isaac, and Jacob.

DEUTERONOMY 29-30

The Torah teaches us that all Jews have promised to obey God's laws. The Torah says that all of us agreed to this covenant, even those of us who had not yet been born. How can this be? The rabbis explain that God took the soul of every Jew who would ever be born and brought all these souls to Mount Sinai so that they would agree to the covenant. Each one of us made a personal promise!

Judaism teaches that if we have done bad things, we cannot excuse ourselves by saying that we never heard God's laws and rules. We cannot say this because the Torah is available to all of us.

On the other hand, although we may know the rules, we may try to use the excuse that we could not control ourselves. But Judaism teaches that we do have the power to choose what we will do. There is no force in the world that can make us be bad against our will or good against our will. It is all up to us. The Torah says, "Choose life!" God has given us the ability to decide whether to be good or bad; whether to obey God's *mitzvot* or disobey them. We have the ability to choose.

Jonah preaches to the people of Ninevah. The story of Jonah teaches that all people can repent and return to God.

Repentance

To repent means to be sorry for the wrongs we have done. Judaism teaches that one can repent at any time, but Yom Kippur is a special day set aside for repentance. The Hebrew word for repentance is *teshuvah* תְּשׁוּבָה. *Teshuvah* means "turning" or "returning." We were going in the wrong direction, but on Yom Kippur we return to the right path. We turned away from God, but now we turn to God. When we turn to God in *teshuvah*, we find that God is turning toward us.

There are three steps to *teshuvah*: confession, regret, and vow. To confess means to admit that we have done wrong. We confess to God all the bad things that we have done in the past year. Jews confess directly to God. The Hebrew word for confession is *vidui* וִדּוּי.

We confess as a group on Yom Kippur. During services we recite two prayers of confession that include long lists of sins. Although no one person could have committed all the sins listed in these prayers, when we confess on Yom Kippur, we speak as one community. As a community we have performed all these sins. There is a special saying:

Kol Yisrael arevim zeh bazeh
כָּל יִשְׂרָאֵל עֲרֵבִים זֶה בָּזֶה, which means "All Israel are responsible for one another." On Yom Kippur we care not only about ourselves but about the entire Jewish community. When we pray as a community, we help one another to walk in God's ways and perform *teshuvah*.

The second step in *teshuvah* is regret. This means that we must be truly sorry for the sins we have committed. For example, if you stole candy from a store,

The liturgical passage "On Rosh Hashanah it is written and on Yom Kippur it is sealed" expresses one of the main ideas of the High Holy Days. During these ten days we turn to God as both the Creator and the Judge of the universe.

you must not be proud that you got away with it or be glad that you were able to enjoy the candy. You must be really sorry that you took something that was not yours.

The final step in *teshuvah* is making a vow. This is the promise we make to do our best never again to repeat a sin. For example, if curiosity made you look at your older sister's private diary, you must convince yourself that you can live without knowing her private secrets. Sure you enjoyed peeking, but you have to decide that you will be strong enough not to do it again!

Teshuvah includes trying to make up for the wrongs we have done. If we stole something, we should return it. If we were mean to someone, we should apologize. If we cannot make up for a sin directly, we should give *tzedakah* and be kind to others. Judaism teaches that God will forgive our sins against other people only if we make peace with them first. No matter what our past misdeeds are, if we sincerely repent, God will always take us back.

High Holy Day services were held at the farm of Moses Bloom in Norwood, New Jersey, in 1919. Although this rural area had no rabbi, people from various communities gathered to hold services together.

Fasting

On Yom Kippur adults fast for twenty-four hours. During that time we do not eat or drink. In addition to refraining from eating and drinking on this day, some Jews also observe other restrictions, which are discussed in the Talmud. The Talmud, which was completed in 500 C.E., is the authorative rabbinic interpretetion of the *Mishnah*. In

Many congregations mark the period of fasting on Yom Kippur by setting up a food bank at the door through which people enter to pray. Congregants donate canned food to the less fortunate on a day when they themselves refrain from eating.

accordance with the solemn spirit of the day, the rabbis prohibited using perfume or makeup, bathing for pleasure (washing oneself for reasons other than health), the wearing of leather shoes, and having physical relations with one's spouse.

We accept these limitations for several reasons. One reason is to humble ourselves before God. Another reason is that on Yom Kippur we aim to be as pure as the angels, who do not eat or drink but only praise God. Our fasting on Yom Kippur also reminds us of other people's sufferings so that we will be moved to help them.

The *haftarah* reading for Yom Kippur morning is from the Book of Isaiah, Chapter 58. In this text Isaiah tells us that God will accept our fasting and prayers on Yom Kippur if we also go out and help the homeless, the poor, and people who are suffering.

> Is this the fast that I look for?… Is this what you call a fast, a day acceptable to *Adonai*? Is not *this* the fast I look for:… to undo the chains of bondage,… to share your bread with the hungry, and to bring the homeless poor into your house? When you see the naked to clothe them and never hide yourself from your own kin,… then shall your light shine in the darkness, and your night become bright as noon.

One year, as my religious school class was preparing for Yom Kippur, I asked each student to let me trace him or her on a big piece of mural paper. Then every student took his or her outline and followed these instructions:

On the *head*, draw something that represents the best idea you had this year or one important thing that you learned.

On the *heart*, draw a picture of the most special feeling that you had this year: good/happy or bad/sad.

On the *legs*, draw a great place that you visited this year.

On the *left hand,* draw a symbol of something about yourself that you'd like to improve.

On the *right hand*, draw a good deed that you did this year.

On the *right shoulder,* show the heaviest burden you've had to carry this past year.

On the *left shoulder,* draw a wish for the coming year.

Everyone in the class felt that these ideas helped us think about both the good and the difficult times we had experienced during the past year. These ideas also helped us explore how Judaism and Yom Kippur encourage us to improve ourselves and the world we live in. And *I* felt that I was starting the new year in a very positive way!

CONNIE R. REITER

THE HEBREW WORD FOR SIN, חֵטְא, COMES FROM ARCHERY. IT REFERS TO MISSING THE TARGET. WHEN AN ARCHER MISSES THE TARGET, HE TRIES TO AIM BETTER AND SHOOTS AGAIN.

What Is Kol Nidre?

Kol Nidre כָּל נִדְרֵי means "All Vows." In the *Kol Nidre* prayer we ask God to forgive us for all the promises we made but were unable to keep. According to one legend, the *Kol Nidre* prayer began with the Marranos, the secret Jews of Spain. In 1492 all the Jews of Spain were ordered to convert to Christianity. Many of them risked their lives to practice Judaism in secret. On Yom Kippur the Marranos gathered in hiding places to chant the *Kol Nidre*. This was their way of telling God that they did not mean it when they promised to give up Judaism.

What makes the *Kol Nidre* so popular today is not only the words of the prayer but its beautiful melody. There are famous cases of Jews who had considered leaving Judaism, but when they came to synagogue on Yom Kippur and heard the *Kol Nidre*, it brought them back to their people and their God. For many Jews today, the most important time of the Jewish year is when the congregation stands, the leaders take all the Torah scrolls out of the ark, and the cantor chants the *Kol Nidre*.

This illustration, created in Europe in the late 1700s, depicts the Kol Nidre *service, held on the eve of Yom Kippur.*

Yom Kippur in the Days of the Temple

In ancient times, when the Holy Temple stood in Jerusalem, Yom Kippur was known as "The Great Day." Jews everywhere turned their eyes and hearts to the Temple, where the High Priest כֹּהֵן גָּדוֹל conducted the sacred ceremonies. During those times, Jews worshiped God by offering sacrifices. In most cases, the sacrifices of the Israelites consisted of food and drink. A portion was roasted and offered to God. Priests offered these sacrifices on behalf of all the people.

On Yom Kippur the High Priest dressed in a white robe and offered many special sacrifices. At one point in the service, two goats were brought before the High Priest. By lottery it was decided which of the two goats would be offered as a sacrifice. The High Priest then tied a red ribbon to the horns of the other goat. This second goat was known as the scapegoat. The High Priest placed his hands on the scapegoat and confessed:

At the time when the Temple stood in Jerusalem, the High Priest would prepare one goat as the sacrifice and one goat as the scapegoat on Yom Kippur.

"O God, I have sinned; I have been unjust; I have transgressed against You, I and Your people, the House of Israel. O God, forgive our sins as it is written in the Torah: 'On this day atonement shall be made for you, to cleanse you. You shall be clean of all your sins before God.'"

And the people answered, "Blessed be the glory of God's kingdom for ever and ever."

One of the priests then led the scapegoat through a gate of the Temple and out into the desert. In this way, the people of Israel symbolically sent away their sins and sought God's forgiveness.

After the year 70 C.E., when the Temple was destroyed, the Jewish people could no longer observe the Yom Kippur service by offering sacrifices in the Temple. Soon after the destruction of the Temple, Rabbi Yochanan ben Zakkai and his student Rabbi Joshua stood gazing at the ruins of the Temple.

"Woe to us!" Rabbi Joshua cried. "The place where Jews were forgiven for their sins is now destroyed."

"My son, do not grieve," replied Rabbi ben Zakkai. "We have another way in which sins can be forgiven. It is to do good for humanity. As it says in Scripture: 'I desire goodness, not sacrifice.'"

SUMMARY

Yom Kippur is the Day of Atonement. It occurs ten days after Rosh Hashanah. It is the conclusion of the ten Days of Awe. We spend the day in the synagogue, atoning for our sins. In addition, most adults fast. However, praying and fasting alone do not automatically lead to *teshuvah*. We must also ask forgiveness of those whom we have wronged. True *teshuvah* is only achieved by admitting our wrongdoings, expressing genuine regret, and promising never to repeat our errors.

In the next chapter we will learn about Sukot, the fall harvest festival that begins on the fifth day after Yom Kippur.

CHAPTER FIVE

SUKOT

There is no finer way of decorating a sukah than seeing to it that the poor do not go hungry.

RABBI HAYYIM HALBERSTAMM OF ZANZ

Sukot
סֻכּוֹת
is celebrated for seven days, beginning on the fifteenth day of the month of Tishri. Sukot, the Feast of Booths, is one of the *Shalosh Regalim*, the "Three Pilgrimage Festivals." Sukot comes on the fifth day after Yom Kippur. We call Sukot *Chag Ha'asif* חַג הָאָסִיף, the "Festival of the Harvest," because we thank God for the autumn harvest. We also call Sukot *Zeman Simchatenu* זְמַן שִׂמְחָתֵנוּ, the "Time of Our Joy." On Sukot we recall how God protected the Israelites during their forty years of travel in the Sinai Desert.

Forty Years in the Desert

After the Israelites were freed from slavery in Egypt, they wandered in the Sinai Desert for forty years. The Sinai Desert was a terrifying place. There was no water, and the land was full of poisonous snakes and scorpions. How could a nation survive in the desert for forty years?

God provided three miracles to help the Israelites survive in the desert. These miracles were a reward for the goodness and faith of Moses and his brother and sister, Aaron and Miriam.

On account of Aaron, God provided a cloud that traveled with the Israelites and covered their heads every day so they would not be burned by the hot sun.

On account of Moses, God provided manna for the Israelites to eat. This manna appeared mysteriously on the ground each morning. The Israelites would go out to collect it. On Friday they would collect a double portion, and on Shabbat they ate what was left over from Friday.

On account of Miriam, God provided a well. The well resembled a rock the size of a beehive, from which water shot high up into the air like a geyser. The well rolled up the mountains with the Israelites and went down into the valleys with them. Wherever Miriam encamped, the well rested close by. The well flowed in all directions throughout Israel's camp, watering the surrounding desert.

When Miriam died, the well sank down into the earth. It is said that the well continues to roll from place to place under the earth. If you take a drink of water at the exact moment that Miriam's Well rolls under your well or reservoir, then you will be drinking from Miriam's Well. That water is the sweetest water in the whole world.

MITZVOT AND MINHAGIM

IT IS A *MITZVAH* TO

- Observe Sukot for seven days, followed by the eighth-day festival called Shemini Atzeret.
- Rejoice during the festival of Sukot.
- Build a *sukah*, an outdoor harvest booth.
- "Live" in the *sukah* during Sukot. We do this by eating at least one meal in the *sukah* during the week of the festival. Some people sleep in the *sukah*.
- Welcome Sukot with a festive meal and by lighting candles and saying *Kiddush* over wine or grape juice.
- Say the blessing for and wave the four species—the *lulav* (palm branch), *etrog* (citron fruit), willow twigs, and myrtle twigs.
- Rest from work on the first day of Sukot and on Shemini Atzeret. The middle days of Sukot, called *Chol Hamoed* חוֹל הַמוֹעֵד, are half-holidays. We try to do only light work on those days.
- Read the biblical Book of Kohelet קֹהֶלֶת—Ecclesiastes—during the festival of Sukot.

IT IS A *MINHAG* TO

- Invite guests into our *sukah*.
- Eat, if you are an Israeli Jew, from the seven species—the seven food crops that God promises in the Torah to provide in the Land of Israel: wheat, barley, figs, pomegranates, grapes, olive oil, and date honey. Jews in Israel also drink freshly squeezed pomegranate juice on Sukot.

War and Peace and the Messianic Age

On the first day of Sukot, we read a *haftarah* from the Book of Zechariah, Chapter 14.

There will come a day that will be not daytime and not nighttime, but there will be light even in the evening…. *Adonai* will be Ruler over all the earth on that day. *Adonai* shall be One and the name of *Adonai* shall be One…. All who remain of all the nations of the world that attacked Jerusalem shall now come each year to worship the Ruler of all creation and to celebrate the festival of Sukot.

The prophet Zechariah was upset that the nations of the world were at war. Just before Zechariah's own lifetime, an army of many nations, led by Babylon, had come and destroyed Jerusalem.

Zechariah believed that God would bring peace among all the nations in the future. On that day, all the nations would celebrate Sukot together.

The world is like a *sukah*. It is a fragile world that is under God's care. We have to share the world in peace so that we can all stand under the roof of our *sukah* and enjoy the earth's good harvest. Sukot challenges the nations of the world to find a way to live in peace. The *sukah* can be seen as a symbol of world peace. Just as a strong wind can demolish a *sukah*, a terrible war could destroy the earth. We have to work together for peace.

The historic signing of the peace treaty by Egyptian President Anwar Sadat (left), Israeli Prime Minister Menachem Begin (right), and American President Jimmy Carter at Camp David. The Camp David Accords was the first peace treaty signed between Israel and an Arab nation.

Building a Sukah

Decorating a sukah *in Israel.*

A *sukah* סֻכָּה is an outdoor booth. In ancient Israel, Jews set up *sukot* in their fields so they could rest during the harvest. The *sukah* should be sturdy enough to withstand strong winds but not be as sturdy as a house. It should feel like a temporary dwelling, a place in which we stop for a while when we are on the move.

A *sukah* has at least three walls. The walls can be made of any material— wood, cloth, or anything else.

The roof is one of the most important parts of the *sukah*. It is temporary, made just for this year's Sukot observance. The roof is constructed completely of natural materials. We usually make a roof by laying boards over the top of the *sukah* and then placing cut branches over the top of the boards. The covering should provide shade from the sun but be open so that the stars can be seen.

To build your own *sukah*, use 2 x 4 boards covered in plywood to make the *sukah* walls. You can drill holes to bolt these boards together or use door hinges to attach them to one another. This method enables you to assemble and take apart your *sukah* each year. You can also make your *sukah* frame from plastic pipe, aluminum fencing poles, or any other material that is easy to use. You can make walls of canvas cloth with holes in the sides to tie the walls to the pipe or poles.

After you have put the walls together and the boards on the roof, you need the *sechach*—the greens for the roof. Cornstalks make good *sechach*. You can also use evergreen branches, willow branches, and clippings from shrubs. Then you can decorate your *sukah*.

Once you have built your *sukah* and are sitting in it, say the following:

בָּרוּךְ אַתָּה, יְיָ אֱלֹהֵינוּ, מֶלֶךְ הָעוֹלָם,
אֲשֶׁר קִדְּשָׁנוּ בְּמִצְוֹתָיו וְצִוָּנוּ לֵישֵׁב
בַּסֻּכָּה.

*Blessed are You, Adonai our God, Ruler of
the universe, who makes us holy with mitzvot
and commands us to dwell in the sukah.*

It is pleasant just to sit in the *sukah*
with friends or with a book. Look up
through the roof. Think about the
beautiful world that God has made for us
and about God's commandment to us to

The arba'ah minim—*the "four species."*

take good care of it.

The Torah tells us to "rejoice" with a
lulav לוּלָב, a beautiful fruit, leafy
branches, and willow branches. (Leviticus
23:40) We call these the *arba'ah minim*
אַרְבָּעָה מִינִים—the "four species."

The *lulav* is a young branch from a date
palm, picked while the leaves are still
tight against the spine of the branch.
When the *lulav* is shaken, the leaves make
a rustling sound.

The beautiful fruit that we use is an
etrog אֶתְרוֹג—a citron. The citron looks
like a lemon. It is oval shaped and has
bright yellow bumpy skin.

The other two species are myrtle twigs
and willow branches. We attach these to
the *lulav* with a braided palm leaf. This
bundle, which includes three myrtle
twigs and two willow branches, is called
the *lulav*, after its largest part.

We rejoice with the four species by
holding them together and waving them
after we have said a blessing. Every
synagogue has a *lulav* and *etrog* for all of
its members to use. It is nice to have a
lulav and *etrog* of your own. Then you
could say the blessing at home each day
during the seven days of Sukot.

To wave the *lulav*, you hold the four
species together in your hands. Usually
we hold the *lulav* in the right hand and
the *etrog* in the left.

Holding the *lulav* and *etrog*, we say the
following blessing:

A religious school teacher teaches a student how to wave a lulav. *The school's* sukah *is in the background.*

בָּרוּךְ אַתָּה, יְיָ אֱלֹהֵינוּ, מֶלֶךְ הָעוֹלָם,
אֲשֶׁר קִדְּשָׁנוּ בְּמִצְוֹתָיו וְצִוָּנוּ עַל
נְטִילַת לוּלָב.

Blessed are You, Adonai our God, Ruler of the universe, who makes us holy with mitzvot and commands us to wave the lulav.

We then wave the *lulav* in six directions: to the front, to the side, to the back, to the other side, up, and down.

There are some interesting explanations for the meaning of the four species.

One meaning is that the four species stand for four kinds of Jews. The *etrog,* with its taste and fragrance, represents those who study Torah and do good deeds. The palm, with its good taste but no smell, is like those who study but do not act. The myrtle, with its smell but no taste, is like those who do good deeds but do not study. The willow, with neither taste nor smell, is like those who neither study nor do good deeds.

When we hold the four species together, we remember that there are all kinds of Jews and that there is a place for all of them among the Jewish people. All Jews should unite as one people, like the four species held together!

DID YOU KNOW THAT THE PILGRIMS IN MASSACHUSETTS CAME UP WITH THE IDEA FOR THANKSGIVING AFTER READING ABOUT THE FESTIVAL OF SUKOT IN THE BIBLE?

Yom Kippur has been over for four days and my daughter Rachel is eager for us to start building the *sukah*. She is in charge of the decorations. First, we put up the frame together. Then, Rachel makes signs that say Happy Sukot! and *Beruchim Habaim* בְּרוּכִים הַבָּאִים—Welcome! We put the signs up on the walls of our *sukah*. Rachel hangs fruit from the ceiling with pieces of string and punches a hole in the top of our Rosh Hashanah greeting cards and hangs them up.

It is a custom to invite friends and relatives to the *sukah*, as well as symbolic guests—fourteen of our great Jewish ancestors, one man and one woman for each of the seven days. This *minhag* is called *Ushpizim* אֻשְׁפִּיזִין—"Invitation." Rachel draws pictures of these special guests: Abraham, Isaac, Jacob, Joseph, Moses, Aaron, and David—the seven men—and Sarah, Rebecca, Rachel, Leah, Miriam, Hannah, and Deborah—the seven women. Rachel also draws pictures of her favorite Jewish heroes. When we sit in the *sukah* and see their faces, we feel as though we are in the presence of all these honored guests.

Every Sukot we have company in our *sukah* for each of the eight days. This year was especially fun because Rachel invited her entire class to the house for a Sukot snack. With a *lulav* and *etrog* in hand, she greeted all our guests and invited them to help decorate the *sukah*. Her classmates created signs, hung up fruit, and made colorful paper chains out of construction paper. Rachel asked her mother and me to lead the *berachot* and to serve the meal. After we ate, there was plenty of time to enjoy being together in the *sukah* and to appreciate the decorations everyone had made.

DR. IRA SCHWEITZER

Rejoicing on a Festival

A painting by contemporary artist Lynne Feldman.

One of the best reasons to celebrate Jewish holidays is to experience the special joy that we call *simchah* שִׂמְחָה. The Torah commands us: "You shall rejoice on your festival, with your son and daughter, your manservant and maidservant, the Levite, the stranger, the orphan, and the widow in your communities." (Deuteronomy, 16:14)

How can we rejoice on a festival as the Torah commands? What if we are feeling sad? The rabbis answered this question by telling us to do happy things, no matter how we feel. The rabbis forbade us from doing sad things during the *Shalosh Regalim*. We may not mourn for the dead on these holidays. If someone dies during a holiday, we wait until the holiday is over before we begin to mourn.

One important part of our *simchah* is that we are happy for a special reason. On Pesach we are happy not only because we are having a pleasant family dinner but also because God took us out of slavery in Egypt. On Sukot we are happy because God continues to care for us, just as God cared for the Israelites when they traveled through the Sinai Desert. During the festivals we should always pay special attention to why we are rejoicing.

Sharing is another important part of *simchah*. A feast that you eat is not a *simchah* unless you share your food with those who are less fortunate than you. The Torah teaches us to rejoice along with the orphans, the strangers, the poor, and all the other people who are in need. There is no *simchah* without *tzedakah*.

Sukot in Ancient Israel

Jerusalem is the Holy City for the Jewish people, the most holy place on the earth. King David made Jerusalem the capital city of the ancient Kingdom of Israel. David's son King Solomon built the beautiful *Bet Hamikdash* בֵּית הַמִּקְדָּשׁ, "Holy Temple," in Jerusalem. All the Jews came to the Holy Temple to worship God, especially on the Three Pilgrimage Festivals of Sukot, Pesach, and Shavuot.

Originally the *Shalosh Regalim* were important harvest times for the farmers in the Land of Israel. Sukot marked the end of the summer harvest. Pesach marked the birth of the lambs and the beginning of the grain harvest. Shavuot marked the end of the grain harvest and the beginning of the fruit harvest. Farmers came to Jerusalem on the *Shalosh Regalim* to bring God's share of the harvest. Sukot was so popular in ancient Israel that Jews simply called it *Hachag* הֶחָג, "The Festival."

This etching, created in Germany in the eighteenth century, depicts the many sukot *that filled the streets and courtyards of ancient Jerusalem during the Feast of Booths.*

SUMMARY

Sukot, the fall harvest festival, begins on the fifth day after Yom Kippur when the moon is full, on the fifteenth day of Tishri. Sukot is one of the Three Pilgrimage Festivals, the *Shalosh Regalim*. In celebration of Sukot, we build a temporary structure called a *sukah* and we wave the *lulav* and *etrog*.

The last day of Sukot is Simchat Torah, a festival of rejoicing with the Torah. We will learn about this holiday in the next chapter.

CHAPTER SIX

SIMCHAT TORAH

Turn the Torah again and again, for everything is in it. Reflect on it and grow with it. Don't turn from it, for nothing is better than it.

PIRKE AVOT 5:22

Simchat Torah
שִׂמְחַת תּוֹרָה

is celebrated after the Sukot festival. On Simchat Torah we finish reading the Torah for the year and start reading it again for the new year. On this holiday we express our joy in Torah study. Simchat Torah marks the end of the fall holidays—Rosh Hashanah, Yom Kippur, and Sukot.

Akiva Learns the Torah

at the bottom of the fall.

"What made that hole?" asked Akiva.

"The water made it by pounding on the rock for many years," his friends told him.

Akiva said, "If water can make holes in rocks, then the Torah can enter even my hard head."

So Akiva went to school and studied. He sat in first grade with his son to learn the *alef-bet*. Everyone made fun of him, but he paid them no mind. Akiva studied for twelve years. At the end of those years, he had twelve thousand students and followers.

Rabbi Akiva became a great teacher. He opened a school outdoors under a fig tree so that everyone—rich and poor—would feel welcome to come and study Torah.

Akiva was a poor shepherd who had never learned to read or write. At the age of forty, he decided that he wanted to study Torah. But Akiva doubted his ability to learn. One day Akiva walked by a waterfall. He noticed a hole in the rock

MITZVOT AND MINHAGIM

IT IS A *MITZVAH* TO
- Celebrate Simchat Torah as a festival day of joy.
- Finish the annual reading of the Torah in the synagogue and immediately begin the annual reading for the coming year.
- Participate in the joy of Simchat

Torah by joining in the procession with the Torah in the synagogue called *hakafot*.

IT IS A *MINHAG* TO
- Welcome new religious school students on Simchat Torah with the ceremony of consecration.

The Cycle of Torah Readings

Every year, from one Simchat Torah to the next, we read the Torah from start to finish. The Torah is arranged into fifty-four portions, one for each Shabbat in the Jewish year. We call this weekly reading the *parashat hashavua* פָּרָשַׁת הַשָּׁבוּעַ, the "weekly portion." On Simchat Torah we finish our annual reading of the Torah by reciting the final verses from the Book of Deuteronomy (34:5-12).

So Moses the servant of God died there, in the land of Moab, at the command of God. God buried him in the valley in the land of Moab, near Beth-peor, and no one knows his burial place to this day. Moses was a hundred and twenty years old when he died. He could still see and he had all his strength. The Israelites mourned for Moses in the plains of Moab for thirty days.

The period of wailing and mourning for Moses came to an end.

Now Joshua son of Nun was filled with the spirit of wisdom because Moses had laid his hands upon him. And the Israelites listened to Joshua.

Never again did there arise in Israel a prophet like Moses, whom God had singled out, face to face, for the many signs and wonders that God sent him to display in the land of Egypt against Pharaoh and all his courtiers and his whole country, and for all the great might and awesome power that Moses displayed before all Israel.

Immediately after this reading, we read the story of creation from the Book of Genesis (1:1–3). Here are the opening verses:

When God began to create the heaven and the earth, the earth was unformed and empty, with darkness over the surface of the deep. And the spirit of God swept over the water. God said, "Let there be light"; and there was light.

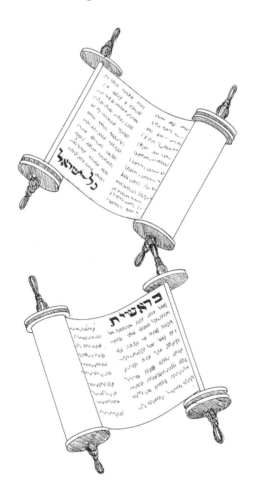

On Simchat Torah we read the final verses of Deuteronomy and the first verses of Genesis.

When we read from the last verses of the Torah and then immediately start a new cycle of annual Torah readings by reading from the first verses of the Torah, we express our commitment to *Talmud Torah* תַּלְמוּד־תּוֹרָה, the "Study of Torah."

Jewish people of every age are part of the Torah. You and your generation will make the Torah your own and decide how you will live by it. Your way of living by the Torah may be different from that of your parents.

Before Moses died, he laid his hands on Joshua. Moses honored Joshua so that the Jews would follow him. When Joshua died, he passed on the leadership and the wisdom of the Torah to the judges, the leaders of the Twelve Tribes of Israel. The judges passed on the Torah to the prophets, and the prophets passed it on to the wise rabbis of old. Every generation has its own leaders who study Torah and teach it. They help us decide how we can best live by the Torah in our own times.

In a way, there are two parts to the Torah. One Torah is composed of the words written in the Torah. The other Torah is the way each generation understands the Torah and passes that understanding on to its children.

Identify a Sefer Torah

In this Torah procession the members of the congregation carry Torah scrolls before taking them back to the bimah.

The Hebrew word for book is *sefer* סֵפֶר. Most books are printed on paper. The letters of a book are printed on the paper by a printing press. The pages are piled one on top of another and glued or sewn together. A cloth or heavy paper cover is put on the book. This is the kind of book with which you are familiar.

Long ago, books were made differently. In ancient Israel books were written on parchment, which is the skin of a sheep or goat. The parchment pages were sewn end to end instead of being piled one on top of the other. The book was then rolled onto two wooden rollers, one at each end.

When we read the Torah in public in the synagogue on Shabbat and holidays, we use a *Sefer Torah* סֵפֶר תּוֹרָה—which is a *sefer* written the old way—that contains the Five Books of the Torah.

The *Sefer Torah* is a symbol of the Jewish commitment to Torah study from generation to generation.

A Sefer Torah *is written by a sofer* סוֹפֵר, *a scribe who is specially trained in the art of Hebrew calligraphy. It usually takes a scribe one full year to complete the writing of a* Sefer Torah.

The Torah Service of Simchat Torah

When it is time for the Torah service, we take every *Sefer Torah* out of the ark. Before we read from the Torah, we parade around the synagogue. The circling of the synagogue with the *Sifre Torah* is called *hakafot* הַקָּפוֹת. Each circle is called a *hakafah*. It is a requirement to make seven *hakafot* around the synagogue.

Leaders of the congregation carry the *Sifre Torah* in the front of the parade. Behind them come the children of the congregation, waving flags. In some congregations the *hakafot* are performed formally. In other congregations the people jump and dance as they carry the Torahs. Some congregations first make one or more "formal" *hakafot*; then they dance with the Torah as long as they like.

After the *hakafot* we put two *Sifre Torah* on the *bimah* and read from each of them. We recite the following blessing before we read from the Torah:

בָּרְכוּ אֶת־יְיָ הַמְבֹרָךְ!
בָּרוּךְ יְיָ הַמְבֹרָךְ לְעוֹלָם וָעֶד!
בָּרוּךְ אַתָּה יְיָ, אֱלֹהֵינוּ מֶלֶךְ הָעוֹלָם,
אֲשֶׁר בָּחַר־בָּנוּ מִכָּל־הָעַמִּים,
וְנָתַן־לָנוּ אֶת־תּוֹרָתוֹ.
בָּרוּךְ אַתָּה יְיָ, נוֹתֵן הַתּוֹרָה.

This painting depicts Simchat Torah at the synagogue in Leghorn, Italy, in 1850.

Blessed are You, Adonai, to whom our praise is due!

Blessed are You, Adonai, to whom our praise is due, now and forever!

Blessed are You, Adonai our God, Ruler of the universe, who has chosen us from all peoples and has given us Your Torah.

Blessed are You, Adonai, Giver of the Torah.

The following is the blessing for after the reading:

בָּרוּךְ אַתָּה, יְיָ אֱלֹהֵינוּ, מֶלֶךְ הָעוֹלָם, אֲשֶׁר נָתַן־לָנוּ תּוֹרַת אֱמֶת, וְחַיֵּי עוֹלָם נָטַע בְּתוֹכֵנוּ. בָּרוּךְ אַתָּה יְיָ, נוֹתֵן הַתּוֹרָה.

Blessed are You, Adonai our God, Ruler of the universe, who has given us a Torah of truth, implanting within us eternal life. Blessed are You, Adonai, Giver of the Torah.

JEWISH FAMILY ALBUM

When I was a child growing up in the Bronx, Simchat Torah was my favorite holiday. I lived in a very Jewish neighborhood. In fact, until I was ten years old, I didn't know there were other religions in the world. I honestly thought that everyone was Jewish!

In those days we celebrated Simchat Torah in the following way. Our mothers got flags with Jewish symbols on them from the hobby shop. The flags were attached to wooden sticks that had pointy, sharp tops. We stuck an apple through the pointy top. Then our mothers hollowed out the apple and put a Shabbat candle in the center. At sundown the rabbi and other community leaders took all the Torahs from the synagogue into the street. Our mothers lit our candles and we danced in the street around the Torahs.

There were hundreds of children (or so it seemed to me), all dancing in the dark with our candles glowing. Then we paraded down the street behind the Torahs with our candles still lit. We danced and sang our love for God, for the Torah, and for each other. We were happy and our candles were so beautiful. It was the most joyous and wonderful time of the year.

SANDY SCHLANGER

Why Do Some Jews Celebrate Simchat Torah on Different Days?

Until the Jewish calendar was calculated and written down, Rosh Chodesh, the beginning of each month, was announced by observers in the Land

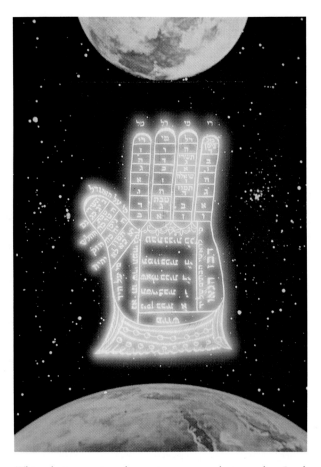

This photo montage by contemporary photographer Jacob Bender uses a Jewish calendar created in Offenbach, Germany, in 1722.

of Israel who watched for the moon to reappear. Then messengers would notify all the Jews in the world that the new month had begun. As you can imagine, this method was not very precise. The rabbis who lived in distant communities could never be sure how much time had passed since the new moon had appeared over Israel. Because of this uncertainty, the rabbis did not know exactly when a holiday began. To be sure the holiday started on the right date, they decided that the first two days of the most important holidays would be observed.

Today, even though we can figure out the exact date of the holidays, many Jews outside the Land of Israel continue to observe an extra day at the beginning and end of many holidays. For example, in the Torah we are instructed to celebrate Sukot for seven days. The first day of Sukot is a holy day on which we are told not to do any work. In order to insure that Jews celebrated the start of Sukot properly, the rabbis decided that the second day of Sukot would also be a holy day.

After Sukot, the Torah instructs us to observe another holy day: Shemini Atzeret שְׁמִינִי עֲצֶרֶת, or the "Eighth Day of Assembly." Shemini Atzeret is also a day for special prayers and no work. Because it was a separate holiday, the rabbis also added a second day to the celebration of Shemini Atzeret. Around the tenth century, this second day became a separate holiday, Simchat Torah. For Jews who observe an extra day of Sukot, Simchat Torah occurs on the ninth day from the beginning of Sukot.

Orthodox and Conservative Jews observe the second and eighth days of Pesach as holy days. Other holidays that are celebrated with an added day are Shavuot and Rosh Hashanah. Other Jews, however, have decided that since we are now certain when the holidays fall, it is no longer necessary to continue observing the second day of the holidays. Most Reform Jews, for example, have returned to observing the number of days of each holiday as written in the Torah. Thus, for example, most Reform Jews celebrate Shemini Atzeret and Simchat Torah on the same day—that is, on the eighth day from the beginning of Sukot.

Synagogues and individuals make their own choices based on the movement of Judaism with which they are affiliated or on their own family customs. What do your synagogue and family observe?

Hallel

On the *Shalosh Regalim* and on Chanukah, we recite *Hallel* הַלֵּל, which is composed of Psalms 113 to 118. The word *Hallel* means "Praise." When we recite *Hallel*, we praise God.

HALLELUJAH! PRAISE GOD!
GIVE PRAISE, O YOU SERVANTS OF
    ADONAI,
PRAISE GOD'S NAME.

GOD RAISES THE POOR FROM
    THE DUST,
AND LIFTS UP THE NEEDY FROM
    THE DIRT
SO THEY SIT WITH PRINCES,
EVEN WITH THE PRINCES OF THEIR
    OWN PEOPLE.

PSALMS 113:1; 7-8

DANCE, O EARTH, BEFORE ADONAI,
AT THE PRESENCE OF THE GOD OF
    JACOB,
WHO TURNED THE ROCK INTO A
    POOL OF WATER,
THE FLINT INTO A FLOWING
    SPRING.

PSALMS 114: 7-8

GIVE THANKS TO ADONAI, FOR
    GOD IS GOOD,
ADONAI'S LOVE IS EVERLASTING.

PSALMS 118: 29

Consecration

We welcome new students to Jewish learning during the ceremony called consecration. Many congregations have a consecration ceremony on Simchat Torah for kindergarten or first-grade students.

The rabbi calls the consecration

Students and teachers at a consecration ceremony in Toronto, Ontario. Each child has received a certificate from the synagogue.

students up to the *bimah*. The children might recite the *Shema* שְׁמַע, their first Jewish lesson. The rabbi asks God to bless the children. The children may receive a certificate and a small toy *Sefer Torah* as a gift. The children may then parade with their little Torah scrolls in the *hakafot*.

In ages past, consecration was held in the spring on Shavuot. Parents dressed their children all in white. The children were then carried to the synagogue on the shoulders of the town's leaders. In the synagogue the children were taught their first Jewish lesson, the name of the Hebrew letter *alef*. Then the children were given a treat. Sometimes it would be a letter *alef* made with honey. Sometimes candy would be dropped onto the children's writing slates. The children would be told that God's angels had sent this candy because they were so happy that the children were beginning to learn Torah.

SUMMARY

On Simchat Torah we complete the yearly cycle of Torah portions by reading from the last portion and then starting over by reading from the beginning of the Torah. We celebrate the holiday by marching and dancing around the synagogue with the Torah in our arms.

Simchat Torah is the last of the fall holidays that occur over a three-week period. After celebrating four holidays in a row, we need a rest! The calendar gives us one. Except for Shabbat, we don't observe any more holidays until Chanukah. We will learn about Chanukah in the next chapter.

CHAPTER SEVEN

CHANUKAH

Through the power of Your spirit, the weak defeated the strong, the few prevailed over the many, and the righteous were triumphant.

LITURGY

Chanukah is the Festival of Lights. It is celebrated for eight days in winter, beginning on the twenty-fifth day of the month of Kislev. On Chanukah we remember the victory of Judah Maccabee over forces of tyranny and the rededication of the Temple in Jerusalem. On this holiday we celebrate religious freedom and we affirm God's saving power.

63

The Origin of Chanukah

Jews whom you find observing Jewish laws and rituals. Force them to violate their Sabbath and bow down to our Greek gods."

Greek soldiers went from town to town. They destroyed synagogues and burned Torah scrolls. They forced Jews to bow down before Greek idols and to break the Jewish dietary laws. In Jerusalem the soldiers entered the Holy Temple and erected a statue of the Greek god Zeus. The Hellenist priests sacrificed pigs on the Temple's altar. During those dark and terrible times, many Jews fled from Jerusalem.

In 175 B.C.E., Antiochus IV became the king of Syria. At that time, Syria was part of the vast Greek Empire. The tiny Land of Israel, then known as Judea, was ruled by Syria.

Antiochus believed that he was the Greek god Zeus incarnate, come to earth as a human. He called himself Antiochus Epiphanes—Antiochus the Divine. His enemies called him Antiochus Epimanes—Antiochus the Madman.

Antiochus tried to force the Jews to assimilate into Greek society and abandon Judaism. Antiochus told his generals, "I order you to put to death all

In 168 B.C.E., a Greek officer led a group of soldiers to the village of Modin near Jerusalem. There they erected an altar to the Greek gods. Then the officer went to Mattathias, who was an elder of the Jewish priesthood. Mattathias had five sons—Johanan, Eleazar, Judah, Jonathan, and Simeon. The Greek officer offered Mattathias money and a noble title if he would be the first to worship idols.

"You may force others to bow to your demands and give up their faith, but I and my family will stay true to the Torah," Mattathias responded and slew the Greek officer. Then he led his sons into the hills of Judah to fight. Mattathias became the leader of the Jewish rebellion.

But Mattathias was old. He could not continue to lead the fight for freedom. When his time came to die, he left his middle son Judah in charge. Judah became known by the nickname Maccabee, "Hammer," because he struck at the enemy like a hammer. For three years Judah Maccabee and his followers fought the Greeks, striking from their hideouts in the hills of Judah. The Jews defeated one Greek army after another. Finally King Antiochus offered the Maccabees a treaty and agreed to let the Jews live in peace.

Judah said to his followers, "Now that our enemies have been crushed, let us go to Jerusalem to purify the Temple and rededicate it."

During the month of Kislev, the Maccabees returned to Jerusalem. Upon entering the Holy Temple, they wept at the sight of the idol of Zeus and the pagan altar. The Maccabees laid down their weapons and began to clean and purify the Temple.

On the twenty-fifth day of the month

After their heroic victory the Maccabees rededicated the Temple as the center of Jewish life.

of Kislev in the year 165 B.C.E., three years after the Greeks had first desecrated the Temple, Judah and his followers rededicated the Temple to God. Judah declared, "Because of the tyranny of Antiochus, we were unable to offer sacrifices in the Temple on the eight days of Sukot. Let us now celebrate our freedom for eight days by lighting the menorah and offering sacrifices."

But when they looked for the special oil to light the lamps of the menorah, they only found a small vial of oil that had the seal of the High Priest. The oil was only enough to relight for one day the menorah that stood in the Temple.

But through a miracle, this oil lasted the whole eight days of the festival.

As Judah Maccabee looked at the flames flickering in the menorah, he declared, "Every year from this time forth, let the Jews in every land celebrate these eight days of Chanukah as a joyous feast in gratitude for God's many miracles." Then Judah Maccabee sent letters to the Jews in every land, telling them of the new holiday and of how God had saved the Jewish people.

MITZVOT AND MINHAGIM

IT IS A *MITZVAH* TO

- Celebrate Chanukah for eight days, beginning on the twenty-fifth day of the month of Kislev.
- Be happy and avoid signs of sadness on Chanukah.
- Light the *chanukiah*, the Chanukah lamp, each night during the eight days of Chanukah and say the proper blessings.
- Play games and enjoy oneself, especially during the time that the Chanukah lights are burning.

IT IS A *MINHAG* TO

- Place the *chanukiah* near a window in order to recall the miracle of Chanukah.
- Play games with a *dreidel*—a four-sided top.
- Eat foods cooked in oil to remember the miracle of the oil. *Latkes*—potato pancakes—and *sufganiot* סֻפְגָּנִיּוֹת— jelly doughnuts—are the most popular.

What Was the Miracle of Chanukah?

The word *Chanukah* means "Dedication." On Chanukah we celebrate the miracle of the rededication of the Temple in Jerusalem. There are two different versions of the miracle of Chanukah. According to the Books of the Maccabees:

> On the very same day that the Greeks profaned the Temple, on the twenty-fifth day of the month of Kislev, the Maccabees finished cleansing the sanctuary. They celebrated for eight days, as on the feast of Sukot, remembering how during Sukot they were wandering in the mountains and living like animals in caves.
>
> II MACCABEES, CHAPTER 10

To the Maccabees, the miracle of Chanukah was the victory of the few over the many. The Talmud, which contains the laws and traditions of the rabbis, gives a different version of the celebration of Chanukah:

> What is Chanukah? Beginning on the twenty-fifth of Kislev, there are eight days with no mourning or fasting because when … the Hasmoneans [the Maccabees] defeated [the Greeks], they searched and found a single vial of oil with the seal of the High Priest on it. It was enough oil to last for one day, but by a miracle it lasted for eight days.
>
> SHABBAT 21B

To the rabbis the story of the miracle of the oil shows that the incredible victory of the Maccabees was possible only because of God's saving power. God was pleased with the Jews, who worshiped God and obeyed the Torah even when they were being persecuted by King Antiochus. Therefore, God made a miracle.

The Talmud was written many years after the time of Chanukah. After the Maccabees succeeded in their revolt, the Romans conquered the Greek Empire. Like the Greeks before them, the Romans also tried to rule over the Jewish people and take away their freedom. The Jews rebelled against the Romans. But this time the few did not defeat the many. The Romans conquered Jerusalem and exiled the Jews from the Land of Israel.

The rabbis who lived after these terrible events did not want Jews to follow the example of Judah Maccabee. The rabbis believed that the Jewish people would return to the Land of Israel not through acts of war but only through God's redeeming power. As it is written in the Torah, "Not by might, not by power, but by My spirit alone [shall you live in peace]." (Zechariah 4:6)

It was not until modern times, about

The Greeks desecrated the Temple.

one hundred years ago, that Jews regained the strength to fight for their rights in the Land of Israel. Jews returned to their homeland to build the new Jewish State of Israel. Jews once again remembered Judah Maccabee as an example of a brave Jew who fought for the freedom of his people. Judah Maccabee's readiness to fight for freedom made God's miracle of the Chanukah vial of oil possible.

THE STORY OF THE MACCABEES IS NOT IN THE HEBREW BIBLE. IT IS TOLD IN THE BOOKS OF THE MACCABEES. THESE WORKS ARE FOUND IN THE *APOCRYPHA*, A COLLECTION OF ANCIENT JEWISH BOOKS THAT WERE NOT INCLUDED IN THE TWENTY-FOUR BOOKS THAT MAKE UP THE HEBREW BIBLE.

Lighting the Chanukiah

The candelabra, or menorah מְנוֹרָה, that Judah Maccabee relit in the Temple in Jerusalem had seven lampstands on it, with an oil lamp on top of each lampstand. The menorah is the symbol of the Jewish people. Today a large bronze menorah stands outside the Knesset כְּנֶסֶת, the government building of modern Israel in Jerusalem.

The Chanukah lamp is not quite the same as a menorah. It has eight branches, one for each night of Chanukah, plus a ninth branch for the *shamash* שַׁמָּשׁ, which is used to light the other lamps. The nine-branched Chanukah lamp is called a *chanukiah* חֲנֻכִּיָה. Jewish artists make a variety of beautiful *chanukiot*. Many Jews proudly display their *chanukiah* in a place where it can be seen all year-round.

The rules for lighting the *chanukiah* are as follows:

- Light one candle on the first night, two candles on the second night, three on the third night, and so on.
- As you face the *chanukiah*, place the candles in the *chanukiah* from right to left, in the same direction in which Hebrew is written.
- Light the candles from left to right so that the candle for the new night is the first candle lit on that night.
- If possible, place the *chanukiah* near a window so that it can be seen from the street.

This mosaic from an ancient synagogue depicts several Jewish symbols, including the menorah, a symbol of the Jewish people.

OUR RABBIS TAUGHT:

- THE *MITZVAH* OF CHANUKAH REQUIRES THAT EACH FAMILY LIGHT ONE LAMP EACH NIGHT. A FAMILY THAT WISHES TO ADD TO THE BEAUTY OF THIS *MITZVAH* SHOULD HAVE EACH MEMBER OF THE HOUSEHOLD LIGHT ONE LAMP ON EACH NIGHT.

BEFORE THE METHOD OF LIGHTING THE *CHANUKIAH* WAS FIXED, TWO DIFFERENT METHODS WERE USED:

- THE SCHOOL OF SHAMMAI TAUGHT THAT EIGHT FLAMES ARE LIT ON THE FIRST NIGHT AND ONE LESS EACH FOLLOWING NIGHT.

- THE SCHOOL OF HILLEL TAUGHT THAT ON THE FIRST NIGHT ONE FLAME IS LIT AND ONE MORE EACH FOLLOWING NIGHT.

THE SCHOOL OF HILLEL'S REASON FOR LIGHTING ADDITIONAL CANDLES EVERY NIGHT IS THAT WE SHOULD INCREASE IN MATTERS OF HOLINESS AND NOT REDUCE.

TODAY WE FOLLOW THE METHOD OF THE SCHOOL OF HILLEL.

Before we light the candle(s), we light the *shamash* and sing the following blessing:

בָּרוּךְ אַתָּה, יְיָ אֱלֹהֵינוּ, מֶלֶךְ הָעוֹלָם, אֲשֶׁר קִדְּשָׁנוּ בְּמִצְוֹתָיו וְצִוָּנוּ לְהַדְלִיק נֵר שֶׁל חֲנֻכָּה.

Blessed are You, Adonai our God, Ruler of the universe, who makes us holy with mitzvot and commands us to kindle the lights of Chanukah.

We light the candle(s) and then sing the following blessing:

בָּרוּךְ אַתָּה, יְיָ אֱלֹהֵינוּ, מֶלֶךְ הָעוֹלָם, שֶׁעָשָׂה נִסִּים לַאֲבוֹתֵינוּ בַּיָּמִים הָהֵם בַּזְּמַן הַזֶּה.

Blessed are You, Adonai our God, Ruler of the universe, who made miracles for our ancestors in days of old at this season.

On the first night of Chanukah, we add the following blessing:

בָּרוּךְ אַתָּה, יְיָ אֱלֹהֵינוּ, מֶלֶךְ הָעוֹלָם, שֶׁהֶחֱיָנוּ וְקִיְּמָנוּ וְהִגִּיעָנוּ לַזְּמָן הַזֶּה.

Blessed are You, Adonai our God, Ruler of the universe, for giving us life, for sustaining us, and for enabling us to reach this season.

We may then recite the following prayer:

We kindle these lights because of the wondrous deliverance You performed for our ancestors in days of old at this season. During the eight days of Chanukah, these lights are sacred. We are not to use them but only to behold them, so that their glow may rouse us to give thanks for Your wondrous acts of deliverance.

It is customary at this time to sing Chanukah songs. A popular hymn for Chanukah is *Maoz Tzur*—"Rock of Ages." Here is one verse in Hebrew and one in English:

מָעוֹז צוּר יְשׁוּעָתִי, לְךָ נָאֶה לְשַׁבֵּחַ, תִּכּוֹן בֵּית תְּפִלָּתִי, וְשָׁם תּוֹדָה נְזַבֵּחַ. לְעֵת תַּשְׁבִּית מַטְבֵּחַ וְצָר הַמְנַבֵּחַ, אָז אֶגְמוֹר, בְּשִׁיר מִזְמוֹר, חֲנֻכַּת הַמִּזְבֵּחַ.

*Rock of Ages, let our song
Praise Your saving power;
You, amid the raging foes,
Were our sheltering tower.
Furious, they assailed us,
But Your arm availed us,
And Your word broke their sword,
When our own strength failed us.*

In many families, gifts are exchanged after the candlelighting ceremony. The family may wish to spend the next half hour in the presence of the candles, playing games, reading stories about Chanukah, and enjoying one another's company.

DURING THE REBELLION AGAINST KING ANTIOCHUS, THE JEWS WOULD NOT FIGHT ON SHABBAT. THE GREEK ARMIES WENT INTO THE HILLS ON SHABBAT, FOUND THE JEWS IN THEIR HIDING PLACES, AND KILLED THEM WITHOUT A STRUGGLE. AS A RESULT, THE MACCABEES MADE A NEW LAW. THEY PERMITTED JEWS TO FIGHT ON SHABBAT IN ORDER TO SAVE THEIR LIVES. "LET US BREAK ONE SHABBAT NOW SO THAT WE MAY FULFILL MANY *SHABBATOT* IN THE FUTURE," SAID THE MACCABEES.

Playing Dreidel

The *dreidel* is a four-sided top. On each side is written one of the letters *Nun, Gimel, Hei, Shin*. These letters are said to stand for the words *Nes Gadol Hayah Sham* נֵס גָּדוֹל הָיָה שָׁם—"A Great Miracle Happened There." You can think of the letters as standing for **N**othing, **G**et, **H**alf, and **S**hare.

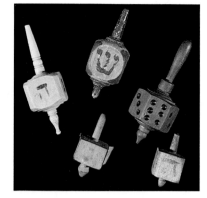

In Israel the dreidel *has* Pei *for* Po, *"Here," instead of* Shin *for* Sham, *"There."*

We can play *dreidel* with nuts, candies, coins, or pebbles. Every player puts a bet into the pot—perhaps two nuts. Then the players take turns spinning the *dreidel*. If *Nun* comes up, **N**othing happens. For *Gimel*, the player **G**ets the whole pot, and the players bet again. For *Hei*, the player takes **H**alf the pot. For *Shin*, the player has to **S**hare, that is, put an extra bet into the pot.

JEWISH FAMILY ALBUM

Growing up, I remember that we lit three *chanukiot*, one for each child in our family. In my home now, we have added to that tradition. We set out many *chanukiot* on the fireplace mantel for eight days. On each night of Chanukah, everyone in our home—adults, children, relatives, and friends—is invited to light a *chanukiah*.

We have quite a collection of *chanukiot*, each with a special significance: a Jerusalem scene that was a wedding gift; a Noah's ark menorah that my daughter received at birth; a colorful metal train menorah that my son was given on his first Chanukah. This year we added the mosaic tile and Play-Doh menorah my daughter created at school.

Behind the mantel is a large wall mirror. As we light each candle, we can see ourselves and the flames reflected in the mirror. This year our five-year-old held the *shamash* for the first time. Our eighteen-month-old watched and smiled with delight as he clutched (unlit) candles in his hand.

As our family grows over the years, I hope the *chanukiot* will fill the mantel.

RABBI BETH H. KLAFTER

Assimilation

The meaning of Chanukah for many Jews living outside Israel has to do with assimilation. Assimilation occurs when a minority group blends into the larger culture. Very often, Jews feel pressure to blend in with their non-Jewish neighbors and to forget that being Jewish is special.

When Antiochus made Jerusalem a Greek city, some Jews were glad. The Greeks were the rulers of the world. They had developed great teachings and beautiful art. Some Jews wanted to act like the Greeks in order to be successful. But were the Jews willing to give up the great teachings of Judaism and start worshiping idols?

Some Jews were. They stayed in Jerusalem during the rebellion and sent their children to Greek schools. The revolt of the Maccabees against the Greeks became a civil war between those Jews who adopted Greek ways and Jews like Mattathias who did not want to lose their Jewish identities.

When the Maccabees finally became the rulers of Judah, they did not reject all the beauty of the Greek world. They kept the Jewish laws and religion, but they borrowed many good ideas from the Greeks. For example, the *yeshivah*, or seminary, in which rabbis are trained is a Jewish version of the Greek school, or academy. Judaism has survived to this day because Jews kept Judaism current with the times. We borrow what is best from the world around us, but we continue to remain loyal to our Jewish beliefs.

Chanukah warns us about the danger

The creator of this imaginative chanukiah, *Mae Shafter Rockland, combined Jewish and American symbols to express her pride in being an American Jew.*

we go. However, Chanukah does provide us with a good opportunity to remind our Christian friends and neighbors that not everyone celebrates Christmas. Invite some non-Jewish friends to share Chanukah with your family!

Chanukah and the story of the Maccabees help us remember that our Jewish identity is a special part of who we are. We might enjoy sharing some Christmas festivities with our non-Jewish neighbors, but we must also guard against assimilation so that the Jewish community does not disappear.

of assimilation. Like the Maccabees, we can decide to keep what is special about being Jewish. Sometimes this is hard to do, especially at Chanukah time when we are reminded of Christmas everywhere During the Chanukah season we remind ourselves and the world around us that the revolt of the Maccabees was the first—but certainly not the last—war in history fought for religious freedom.

SUMMARY

Chanukah, the Festival of Lights, begins on the twenty-fifth of Kislev, when the winter days are short and the lights of the *chanukiah* bring cheer into our homes. During this happy festival we recall the victory of the Maccabees and the rededication of the Temple in Jerusalem.

Chanukah lasts for eight days. On each night we bless the lights of the *chanukiah*, adding one candle for each day. Many families exchange gifts, play *dreidel*, and eat potato *latkes*.

The next holiday we will learn about is Tu Bishevat, the New Year for Trees.

CHAPTER EIGHT

TU BISHEVAT

On the sixth day of creation, God said, "See, I give you every seed-bearing plant that is upon all the earth and every tree that has seed-bearing fruit; they shall be yours for food."

GENESIS 1:29

Tu Bishevat

ט"וּ בִּשְׁבָט

is the New Year for Trees. Tu Bishevat is Hebrew for the fifteenth day of the month of Shevat. This holiday falls in late winter, one month before Purim. It is a day to thank God for the bounty of trees and plants that give us food. On Tu Bishevat we plant trees in Israel and appreciate the importance of caring for our environment.

Two for Tu Bishevat

A nomad was traveling in the desert. Hungry, weary, and thirsty, she came upon a tree. Its fruits were sweet, its shade was pleasant, and a stream of water flowed beneath it. She ate of the fruits, drank of the water, and rested under the shade. When she was ready to continue on her way, she asked, "Tree, O Tree, how shall I bless you? Shall I say, 'May your fruits be sweet?' They are sweet already. Shall I say, 'May your shade be pleasant?' It is already pleasant. Shall I say, 'May a stream of water flow beneath you?' A stream of water already flows beneath you. Therefore, I say, May it be God's will that all the shoots taken from you be like you."

TU BISHEVAT IS A SHORT FORM FOR THE FIFTEENTH OF SHEVAT. *TET* EQUALS 9 AND *VAV* EQUALS 6. WE PUT THEM TOGETHER TO MAKE THE WORD *TU* ט״ו, WHICH EQUALS 15.

THIS DAY IS ALSO CALLED *CHAG HA'ILANOT* חַג הָאִילָנוֹת, THE "FESTIVAL OF THE TREES," AND *CHAG HAPEROT* חַג הַפֵּרוֹת, THE "FESTIVAL OF THE FRUIT."

In the time when the Romans ruled over the Jewish people in the Land of Israel, an old man planted a fig tree. A Roman general happened to pass by. He laughed at the old man and said, "You Jews are stupid. Don't you realize it will take twenty years before that tree will grow enough to give fruit, and you will be long dead by then?"

The old man answered, "When I was a small child, I could eat fruit because those who came before me planted trees. Shouldn't I do the same thing for the children who come after me?"

The general said, "If you live long enough to eat figs from this tree, let me know."

In a few years the trees produced figs, and the old man lived long enough to enjoy them. He filled a basket with figs and took them to the general, who honored him.

The general's servants were amazed that he would show honor to a Jew, but the general told them, "His Creator honors him with long life and beautiful trees. I should honor him, too."

LEVITICUS RABBAH 25:5

MITZVOT AND MINHAGIM

IT IS A *MITZVAH* TO
• Celebrate Tu Bishevat.

IT IS A *MINHAG* TO
• Plant trees in the Land of Israel. If we are in Israel, we can plant a tree with our own hands. Jews in America can give money to the Jewish National Fund, which plants trees all over the Land of Israel. You can also plant a tree at home.
• Eat fruit on Tu Bishevat, especially the seven species named in the Bible (Deuteronomy 8:8), which are considered native to the Land of Israel. *Bokser*—carob—is especially associated with Tu Bishevat.
• Have a Tu Bishevat *seder*.

Caring for God's Creation

Families of recent Russian olim, *immigrants to Israel, plant trees in a JNF forest.*

Jewish tradition has many texts about trees, nature, and protecting our world. The following is a small selection of texts to study:

> From the very beginning of creation, the Holy One was occupied with the planting of trees. As it is written, "God planted a garden in Eden."
>
> GENESIS 2:8

> You, too, when you enter the Land, must occupy yourselves first with nothing else but planting trees. As it is said, "When you come into the Land, you shall plant … trees."
>
> LEVITICUS RABBAH 19:23

The Holy One said to Israel, "Even though you will find the Land full of goodness, don't say, "We will sit and not plant." Rather be careful to plant trees. Just as you found trees that others had planted, so you should plant for your children. No one should say, "I am old. How many more years shall I live? Why should I be troubled for the sake of others?" Just as you found trees, you should add more by planting, even if you are old.

MIDRASH TANCHUMA, KODASHIM 8

There is a tradition that at the birth of a girl, a cypress tree is planted, and at the birth of a boy, a cedar tree is planted. When a couple is married, they stand under a *chupah* made of wood from the trees planted at their birth. GITTIN 57A

Rabban Yohanan ben Zakkai used to say, "If you hold a sapling in your hand and are told that the Messiah is here, you should first plant the sapling. Then go out to greet the Messiah."

AVOT DE-RABBI NATAN, CHAPTER 31

When God led Adam through the garden of Eden, God told him, "I made My beautiful and glorious world for your sake. Take care not to hurt or destroy My world for if you do, there is no one to fix it after you."

ECCLESIASTES RABBAH 7

When you go to war against a city and you surround it to capture it, you must not destroy its trees with your axes. You may eat their fruit, but you may not cut them down. Are trees people, who can run away from you into the city? DEUTERONOMY 20:19

According to our sages, the commandment *Bal Tashchit* בַּל תַּשְׁחִית—"Do Not Destroy"—

teaches us that we may not destroy anything that is good and useful.

At the dawn of creation, God placed Adam in the garden of Eden to till it and tend it. From this we learn that God has commanded humankind to take care of the world and everything in it. God has appointed us to be the stewards of the world. A steward is a person whose job it is to watch over and care for property. If we harm or destroy the world or the species that live in it, we are not doing our job as stewards of God's creation. Tu Bishevat reminds us of our responsibility to care for the world that God has created.

Etz chayim, *"tree of life," is a phrase from the Book of Proverbs that has been made into a song. The chorus is, "It is a tree of life to them that hold fast to it and all of its supporters are happy." The tree of life is a symbol for the Torah.*

Celebrate a Tu Bishevat Seder

Preschoolers take part in a Tu Bishevat seder.

The *seder* סֵדֶר for Tu Bishevat is a celebration of God's creation and of the good things that trees give us to eat. Through our Tu Bishevat *seder* we thank God for all the beauty and fertility of the world.

The Tu Bishevat *seder* is not commanded in the Torah. In the 1500s the Jews of Safed created this *minhag*, modeled after the Pesach *seder*. This custom spread among Sephardic Jews, who held a "festival of fruits," during which they ate fifteen kinds of fruits and drank four cups of wine. One tradition is that we drink white wine, white wine mixed with a bit of red, red wine mixed with a bit of white, and pure red wine.

The four colors are a symbol of the four seasons. Grape juice may be used instead of wine.

Part of the fun of the Tu Bishevat *seder* is to see how many different kinds of fruits and nuts we can eat. Some Jews try to enjoy fifteen different types of fruits at their *seder*. Some try to have fifty different types!

Besides different species, we might use fruit prepared in different ways. For instance, we could use fresh fruits, dried fruits, and fruit juice. Some Jews divide their fruits for Tu Bishevat into fruits with shells or rinds, fruits with pits, and fruits that can be eaten whole.

To hold a Tu Bishevat *seder*, we set a table with fruits, wine, and a loaf of bread. We read a selection of prayers, poems, and blessings in a book called a *haggadah* הַגָּדָה. The blessing over fruit is included, usually at least four times:

בָּרוּךְ אַתָּה, יְיָ אֱלֹהֵינוּ, מֶלֶךְ הָעוֹלָם,
בּוֹרֵא פְּרִי הָעֵץ.

Blessed are You, Adonai our God, Ruler of the universe, who creates the fruit of the tree.

The Jewish National Fund

The Jewish National Fund was created in 1901 to purchase and develop land in the Land of Israel. In Hebrew this agency is called *Keren Kayemet Leyisrael* קֶרֶן קַיֶמֶת לְיִשְׂרָאֵל, the "Fund for the Establishment of Israel."

In 1901 the Land of Israel was known as the province of Palestine in the Turkish Empire. The Jewish National Fund purchased land from landowners. It then prepared the land for the establishment of Jewish farms and villages. Most of the new settlements were in the lowlands, where few other people lived because of the swamps that caused malaria and other diseases.

The JNF had to make the land fertile and useful so that it could support a large population of Jewish settlers. The JNF drained swamps and built roads. Its main job, however, was to plant trees. Over the years, the JNF has created large forests in Israel. These forests cool the air, help to attract rain, hold in water, and make the land fertile.

Since 1901, Jews all over the world have kept a little "blue box" in their homes to collect money for the JNF. When the box is filled with coins, we empty it and send the money to the JNF. In this way Jews everywhere can help build up the Land of Israel.

For a few dollars the JNF will plant a tree in your name in the Land of Israel. Each year at Tu Bishevat, the JNF sends collection envelopes to Jewish religious

Yitzhak Rabin, prime minister of Israel, gives tzedakah *to the JNF.*

schools in America so that the students can buy trees. You can also buy a tree in honor or memory of someone. The JNF will send a certificate to the person or family you have chosen to honor to let them know about your generous gift.

Some forests in Israel are named for famous people. You can request that your tree be planted in a forest that is named for someone you admire.

IN ANCIENT TIMES TU BISHEVAT DIVIDED ONE YEAR FROM ANOTHER FOR TITHING THE PRODUCE OF TREES, SO THAT FARMERS COULD CONTRIBUTE ONE-TENTH OF THE FRUIT FOR THE TEMPLE.

Even before the establishment of the State of Israel, Jews all over the world contributed to the JNF. This tzedakah *box was used by Polish Jews in 1920.*

A JNF forest at Lahav in the Negev.

The Chalutzim in Eretz Yisrael

After the Romans destroyed the Second Temple, they forced most Jews to leave the Land of Israel. Israel fell into the hands of empires that ruled it from afar—the Byzantines, the Arabs, the Crusaders, the Turks, and many others. Throughout this time, a small Jewish community continued to live in Israel.

In 1881 more Jews began coming back to *Eretz Yisrael* אֶרֶץ יִשְׂרָאֵל to rebuild the land. The Jewish settlers called themselves *chalutzim* חֲלוּצִים— "pioneers." Among these pioneers were David and Sarah Steinberg. They helped start *kibbutzim* קִבּוּצִים, collective farms or settlements, in the Hula Valley. In 1960 on Tu Bishevat, they recalled their early years in the Land of Israel.

SARAH: When we came to Israel in 1905, this land was part of the Turkish province of Palestine. The Turks had cut down most of the trees years before to build the railroad. The Arabs' flocks overgrazed the land. The hills were desert, and the lowlands were swamp.

DAVID: The first thing we did when we arrived here was plant trees. Trees dry up the swamps and keep the dry lands cool and moist. Wherever Jews settled in those days, they planted trees. That was the sign of the *chalutz*. There was a story that an Arab sheik said to his son, "Learn to get along with these people because people who plant trees are here to stay."

SARAH: Our leader was a man named A. D. Gordon. He was older than the other kibbutzniks. He told us that if we planted trees, we Jews would become

Chalutzim *working in the fields.*

83

A. D. Gordon, who made aliyah to Palestine in 1904, strongly encouraged Jews to plant trees, work the land, and become self-sufficient.

planted in the soil of our land. This would give new spirit and a new life to Jews everywhere.

DAVID: We wanted to make a difference with our lives. The Jewish land needed the Jewish people to make it fertile once again. There is a legend that the Land of Israel was waiting these two thousand years, waiting for her children to come back. Until we came back, the land was sad, like a mother who had lost her children, and that is why the land turned to desert. But now the land is happy again.

SARAH: There are many paths to God. We can find God in the holy books of our people. But when a Jew tills the land, plants a tree, and eats the fruit of that tree … that, too, is a path to God.

SUMMARY

Tu Bishevat, the New Year for Trees, is celebrated on the fifteenth of Shevat. The holiday has ancient origins. Today's celebration of the trees and the environment has evolved over the centuries. One observance is the Tu Bishevat *seder*, created by rabbis during the sixteenth century. At a Tu Bishevat *seder*, people usually eat a variety of different fruits and drink four cups of wine or grape juice. Another important custom of Tu Bishevat is planting trees both in Israel and at home.

In the next chapter of this book, we will learn about Purim, a holiday of merriment and triumph.

CHAPTER NINE

P U R I M

Then the Jews had light and joy, gladness and honor.

ESTHER 8:16

Purim פּוּרִים is celebrated on the fourteenth day of the month of Adar in late winter, one month before Pesach. On Purim we read the Scroll of Esther, *Megillat Esther*, which recounts Queen Esther's victory over the evil tyrant Haman. Purim is a time for fun—for eating, drinking, carnivals, plays, and gifts of food to our friends and to the poor.

Queen Esther and Mordecai

In the days of King Ahasuerus of Persia—this was King Ahasuerus who ruled over 127 provinces from India to Ethiopia—the king gave a great feast in the castle in the capital of Shushan. The king became drunk and ordered Queen Vashti to appear before the crowd. Vashti was giving a feast for the women, and she refused to appear. King Ahasuerus's advisers told him to send the queen away and choose another in her place. He followed their advice.

Queen Vashti refuses to obey King Ahasuerus.

After these things, Ahasuerus sent for beautiful women to come to Shushan from throughout the kingdom so that a new queen could be chosen.

There was a certain Jew named Mordecai, who lived in Shushan. Mordecai had adopted his beautiful niece Esther and raised her as a daughter. At Mordecai's suggestion, Esther went to the king's castle. She found favor above all the other women, and she was made queen. She did not tell the king that she was a Jew, for so Mordecai had instructed her.

In the meantime, two of King Ahasuerus's servants, Bigthan and Teresh, were plotting to kill the king. Mordecai heard of the plot and told Esther about it. Esther, in turn, told the king. In this way, Mordecai saved the king's life, and the deed was written down in the royal records.

Some time later, the king promoted Haman and made him prime minister. Everyone was ordered to bow down to Haman, but Mordecai refused. Haman was very angry. The king's courtiers told Haman that Mordecai was a Jew. Haman decided not only to take revenge on Mordecai but also to do away with all the Jews in the kingdom. Haman cast lots, called *purim*, and chose the fourteenth day of the month of Adar as the day to destroy the Jews.

Then Haman said to King Ahasuerus,

"There is a people scattered among the other peoples of your kingdom whose laws are different from those of everyone else, and they do not obey the king's laws. It is not in Your Majesty's interest to put up with them. If you will issue an edict to destroy them, I will pay ten thousand coins of silver into the king's treasury."

The king said, "You may keep the money, and you may do as you like with these people."

So an edict was sent to every province that on the fourteenth day of the month of Adar, the people could destroy, massacre, and exterminate all the Jews and take their possessions. The king and Haman then sat down to drink, but the city of Shushan was shocked.

When Mordecai heard about these things, he sent for Esther and told her everything. "Do not imagine that you will escape," he said, "because you are in the king's palace. If you keep silent, someone else will save the Jews but you will perish. It may be that you became queen for this very reason."

Esther ordered all the Jews of Shushan to fast and pray with her for three days. Then she said, "Even though it is against the law for anyone, even the queen, to visit the king without being invited, I will go and speak with him. And if I die, I die."

When Esther entered the inner court of the king's house, Ahasuerus was pleased to see her. He said, "What is your request? Even up to half my kingdom, it will be given to you."

Esther replied, "I desire only that you and Haman come to a feast today that I have prepared for you."

The king and Haman went to the feast. The king said to Esther, "What is your request? Even up to half my kingdom, it shall be granted to you." But because Esther was afraid to say what was on her mind, she invited them to another feast the next day.

Haman went home happy. He told his wife Zeresh how the queen had honored him by inviting only him to a banquet with the king. "But," he said, "it spoils my pleasure to see that Mordecai still lives." Zeresh suggested to Haman that he build a gallows fifty cubits high on which

This panel from a Scroll of Esther, created in Italy in the early 1700s, depicts Mordecai riding through the streets of Shushan.

to hang Mordecai. Haman ordered the gallows to be built.

That night, the king could not sleep. He ordered his records to be read to him. When he heard how Mordecai had saved his life and had not yet received a reward, he decided to do something about this matter first thing the next morning.

The next day, Haman intended to seek permission from the king to hang Mordecai from the gallows. The king sent for Haman and asked, "What should be done for a man whom the king is pleased to honor?"

Haman thought to himself, "The king must mean me!" And so he said, "Let that person be dressed in the royal robes, seated on the royal horse, and led through the streets while everyone proclaims, 'This is what is done for the one whom the king wishes to honor.'"

"Splendid!" said the king. "Do all of this for Mordecai the Jew, and you your-self shall lead him through the city." Even though Haman hated Mordecai, Haman did as the king commanded.

That night, Haman and the king went to Queen Esther's banquet. At the banquet the king asked Esther, "What is your request? Even up to half my kingdom, it shall be granted to you."

Esther replied, "If I have found favor in your sight, all I ask is that you spare my life and the lives of my people. We are

about to be destroyed because of an evil tyrant."

King Ahasuerus shouted, "Who would dare to harm you?"

"The adversary and the enemy," replied Esther, "is this wicked Haman!"

The king was furious. He ordered that Haman be hanged on the very gallows that Haman had prepared for Mordecai. Since King Ahasuerus could not undo an edict once it was written, he composed a new edict to save the Jews: On the thirteenth day of Adar, the Jews were given the right to fight for their lives and

Esther accuses Haman of plotting against the Jews of Shushan.

attack anyone who tried to destroy them. So the Jews defeated their enemies. The governors of every province showed kindness to the Jews out of respect for Mordecai. And Mordecai was raised to the position of prime minister, which had been held by Haman.

In the city of Shushan, the king gave the Jews an extra day to fight their foes. On the day after the battle, all the Jews rested. They made the fourteenth day of Adar a day of feasting and merrymaking.

Mordecai and Esther wrote down all that had happened. They sent a message to the Jews throughout the kingdom that from then on, they should celebrate the fourteenth day of Adar as a day of feasting and merrymaking, of sending gifts to one another and presents to the poor.

King Ahasuerus ruled for many years. Mordecai was second in rank to the king. He was much loved by the whole nation. He worked for the good of his people, seeking peace throughout the land.

ADAPTED FROM THE SCROLL OF ESTHER

MITZVOT AND MINHAGIM

IT IS A *MITZVAH* TO

• Observe Purim on the fourteenth day of the month of Adar. In leap years Purim is observed on the fourteenth day of II Adar. In walled cities, such as Jerusalem, Purim is observed one day later, on the fifteenth of Adar. This day is called *Shushan Purim* שׁוּשַׁן פּוּרִים. On Purim, work is permitted; we may not fast or be sad on this day.

• Attend a public reading of *Megillat Esther* on the eve of Purim.

• Send gifts of tasty food to our friends and to the poor. This practice is called *Shalach Manot*—"Sending Portions."

• Rejoice on Purim.

IT IS A *MINHAG* TO

• Drown out the name of Haman during the reading of the *Megillah* with a *gragger*—a noisemaker.

• Wear a costume.

• Make *hamantaschen*—"Haman's hats"—to eat on Purim. These are triangle-shaped pastries filled with fruit.

• Stage a *Purimspiel*—a Purim play.

• Hold a Purim carnival.

Remember Amalek

In preparation for Purim, we study a special Torah portion about Amalek. Amalek was the name of a tribe of nomads. When the Israelites started out on their journey through the Sinai Desert, the Amalekites attacked the Israelites. The Israelites successfully defended themselves against the tribe of Amalek.

The Book of Esther tells us that the evil Haman descended from a king of Amalek named Agog. The Torah tells us that as the Israelites prepared to enter the Promised Land, Moses warned them about the evil of Amalek.

Remember what Amalek did to you on your journey, after you left Egypt. How, unmoved by fear of God, Amalek surprised you on the march. When you were famished and weary, Amalek cut down all the stragglers in your rear. Therefore, when *Adonai* your God grants you safety from all your enemies around you, in the land that *Adonai* is giving you as a hereditary portion, you shall blot out the memory of Amalek from under heaven. Do not forget!

DEUTERONOMY 25:17–19

The name of Amalek is a symbol for evil in the world. The rabbis teach that as long as Amalek exists, peace will never be achieved.

Moses holds his hands high, while Joshua leads the Israelites in battle against the tribe of Amalek. "Whenever Moses held up his hand, Israel prevailed; but whenever he let down his hand, Amalek prevailed." (Exodus 17: 11)

Megillat Esther
The Scroll of Esther

This richly decorated Megillat Esther *was created in the Balkans in the late 1600s.*

same. There is one place where the words are written in very large script. This is the section in which the names of the ten sons of Haman are listed. It is a tradition to read this list in one breath. As the *Megillah* is read in public on the eve of Purim, the children make noise with their *gragger* each time they hear the name of Haman.

A *megillah* מְגִלָּה, which means "scroll," is written by hand on parchment, just like a *Sefer Torah*. A *megillah* is not very long Because a *megillah* is short, we roll it up into a single roll.

Megillat Esther מְגִלַּת אֶסְתֵּר is the most unusual book in the Bible because it does not mention God's name even once. For this reason, Scrolls of Esther are often highly decorated. None of the other books in the Bible are illustrated or decorated because of the fear that the artist might try to depict the image of God.

A panel from a *Megillat Esther* looks very much like a panel from a *Sefer Torah*. As in the Torah, not every column of text looks the

ESTHER HAD A SECULAR NAME AND A HEBREW NAME, JUST AS MANY JEWS TODAY HAVE. ESTHER'S HEBREW NAME WAS HADASSAH. THE WOMEN'S ORGANIZATION HADASSAH IS NAMED FOR HER.

These girls, dressed in costumes for Purim, have their gragger ready to drown out the name of Haman whenever his name is read.

Shalach Manot

The Book of Esther (9:22) tells us that we should send gifts to friends and to the poor on Purim. We call these gifts *Shalach*

Preparing for a Purim party, religious school students carry a tray of hamantaschen *to the oven.*

Manot שָׁלַח מָנוֹת—"Sending Portions." In past times, Purim, not Chanukah, was the time of gift giving. On Purim, Jews might contribute with extra generosity to funds that feed the poor. Jews also give gifts of food—candy and *hamantaschen*—to their friends and neighbors.

Today Judaica shops sell little decorated boxes or bags for *Shalach Manot*. It is fun to bake *hamantaschen*, add some candy and other special treats and maybe a small bottle of wine for adults, and give *Shalach Manot* to our friends and neighbors. Some Jews take *Shalach Manot* to a hospital or nursing home for the Jewish patients. A friendly visit and some goodies make a very fine Purim present.

JEWISH FAMILY ALBUM

My whole family and I dress up in costumes to go to synagogue on Purim. Everyone else at *shul* is dressed up, too. Most people dress up as the characters in the Purim story, but some are also farmers, angels, cats, and mice. Once someone dressed up as a tube of toothpaste. We have services and the rabbi leads as we sing songs with lively melodies. The favorite moment of

Students in a Purimspiel *portray guests at the feast of King Ahasuerus.*

our whole congregation, however, is the *Purimspiel*.

Once I played Esther in the *Purimspiel*. I think she is someone we can be very proud of because she stood up for all Jews when she told the king that she was Jewish. Playing Esther was a lot of fun. It's not every day that a person gets to marry a king and save the Jewish people!

KAREN WIERZBA

Anti-Semitism

People like Haman have appeared thoughout history. He is the anti-Semite, the person who hates Jews. Other such enemies of the Jews include the Greek emperor Antiochus IV; the Roman emperor Hadrian; King Ferdinand and Queen Isabella of Spain; Bogdan Chmielnicki, the Cossack leader in Russia; and Adolf Hitler in Nazi Germany. They all sounded like Haman: "There is a certain people that is different from all others. We should not put up with them...."

Why have the Jews faced so many enemies throughout history? One reason is that we stand up for our belief in God and for what is right. Because we speak up, we are the enemy of all tyrants.

Another reason is that in most places, we are a minority. In countries where everyone is forced to have the same religion or hold the same political views, Jews stand out because we have different beliefs. Religious prejudice also plays a part. Some religious leaders throughout history have spread falsehoods about Jews.

Often people who are not successful in life look for someone to blame other than themselves. They might choose to blame the Jews. Throughout history, Jews have been blamed for the ills of society. This is called scapegoating.

Purim reminds us that we must always be aware of our enemies and the power they have. Purim also teaches us that if we are proud to be Jews, if we stand up for ourselves, and if we act bravely to defend ourselves, as Esther and Mordecai did, then we have the power to defeat our enemies. Anti-Semites have done terrible things to us, but we are still here, one of the most ancient nations on earth. We have much to be proud of. When our enemies fall, we will still be here, celebrating Purim. *Am Yisrael chai* עַם יִשְׂרָאֵל חַי—the people Israel lives!

The cast of a Purimspiel *at the Bais Yaacov School in Kolbuszowa, Poland, in 1938, at the beginning of the Holocaust.*

Purim in Israel Today

Purim is a fun day for everyone in Israel. The day before Purim, children have costume parties in school. At night, families go to hear the reading of *Megillat Esther*. There are Purim specials on television. Children do not attend school on Purim, but stores and businesses are open. Street performers, like clowns and jugglers, appear on street corners and in pedestrian malls. Proud parents and grandparents take their beautifully costumed children walking on the main streets. Queen Esther is still the most popular costume for girls. Boys in Israel like to dress up as spacemen or cowboys.

In Israel you could celebrate Purim twice if you wanted to. Jerusalem, a walled city, celebrates Shushan Purim on the fifteenth of Adar. The rest of the country celebrates Purim on the fourteenth of Adar.

A Purim parade in Israel. Can you guess which three characters in the Purim story these floats represent?

SUMMARY

Purim is a joyous festival that is celebrated on the fourteenth of Adar. We read *Megillat Esther* at services. When we hear the name of Haman, the villain of the story, we drown out his name by making a lot of noise. Purim teaches us that we must stand up for our religious freedom so that no enemy will ever succeed in destroying us.

In the next chapter we learn about the holiday of Pesach, the spring Festival of Freedom.

CHAPTER TEN

P E S A C H

*God saved Israel from slavery on account of four **mitzvot** that Israel observed in Egypt: They kept their Jewish names; they learned the Hebrew language; they were all friends with one another; they did not give up their Jewish customs.*

AFTER THE *MIDRASH*

Pesach
פֶּסַח

is one of the *Shalosh Regalim*. It is a week-long festival beginning on the fifteenth of Nisan, in the spring. Pesach is also called *Zeman Cherutenu* זְמַן חֵרוּתֵנוּ, the "Season of Our Freedom." On Pesach we celebrate the Israelites' Exodus from Egypt. We remember that we were slaves and that God set us free. We look forward to a time when all people will be free.

The First Pesach in Egypt

In the days when the Israelites lived in slavery in Egypt, God sent Moses to Egypt to tell Pharaoh, king of Egypt, "Let my people go." When Pharaoh would not let Israel go, God sent nine plagues against the Egyptians, but still Pharaoh was stubborn.

God called to Moses and said, "I am sending one more plague against the Egyptians. This time, Pharaoh will not only let you go, he will beg you to leave. Toward midnight, I will strike down every first-born in Egypt." Then God commanded Moses to tell the Israelites how to prepare for that night.

Moses summoned all the elders of Israel and said to them, "Go, pick out lambs for your families, and slaughter the passover offering. Take a bunch of hyssop, dip it into the blood that is in the basin, and apply some of the blood ... to the lintel and to the two doorposts. None of you shall go outside the door of his house until morning. For when *Adonai* goes through to smite the Egyptians, God will see the blood on the lintel and the two doorposts, and God will pass over the door and not let the Destroyer enter and smite your home.

"You shall observe this as an institution for all time, for you and your descendants.... And when your children ask you, 'What do you mean by this rite?' you shall say, 'It is the passover sacrifice to *Adonai*, because God passed over the houses of the Israelites in Egypt when

This page of a haggadah *illustrates the first five plagues:* dam—*blood;* tzfardea—*frogs;* kinim—*lice;* arov—*wild beasts; and* dever—*cattle disease.*

God smote the Egyptians but saved our houses.'"

The Israelites did as Moses told them, and they observed the passover sacrifice. They ate the roasted lamb in their homes, with bitter herbs and unleavened bread. They had to be dressed for travel as they ate, with their walking sticks in hand, their cloaks belted up, and their sandals on their feet.

That night, there was crying and sorrow from one end of Egypt to the other, but all the Israelites were safe. Pharaoh called Moses to him. "Leave Egypt, you and all your people!" he said. "Take your families and your flocks, and go worship your God!"

The Israelites left Egypt the next morning in a great hurry. They had no time to let their bread rise, so they baked their bread unleavened and packed it for their journey.

The Israelites' final night in Egypt was the night of the first Pesach, a "night of watching," to be observed by Jews for all time.

ADAPTED FROM EXODUS 3-12

MITZVOT AND MINHAGIM

IT IS A *MITZVAH* TO
- Observe Pesach for seven days, from the fifteenth through the twenty-first day of the month of Nisan. On the first day of Pesach, the first full moon of spring usually appears.
- Eat *matzah*—unleavened bread—and refrain from eating any *chametz*—leavened bread.
- Clean your house from top to bottom just before Pesach to be sure there is no *chametz* in it.
- Participate in the Pesach *seder* and read from the *haggadah*.
- Refrain from working on the first and last days of Pesach and do only light and pleasant work during the week of Pesach.
- Give *tzedakah* before Pesach.

IT IS A *MINHAG* TO
- Eat foods that are special for Pesach during the week of the festival. These include *matzah brie* (also called fried *matzah*), macaroons, and *matzah* meal pancakes.
- Wear your new spring clothes for the first time during Pesach, in honor of the holiday.
- Invite some non-Jewish friends to participate in the *seder*.

Crossing the Sea of Reeds

The Sea of Reeds closes over Pharaoh's army.

The Torah portion for the last day of Pesach tells us how the Israelites crossed the Sea of Reeds on dry land after they left Egypt. But then Pharaoh changed his mind: He no longer wanted to let the Israelites go. He sent his army after them. As the Egyptian army chased the Israelites, the waters closed over the Egyptians and drowned them.

After the Israelites crossed the sea, they sang a song of thanks to God, which is called the "Song at the Sea." It is found in the Torah in Exodus 15:1-19.

I will sing to *Adonai*, for God has won a great victory;
Horse and driver God has thrown into the sea.
Adonai is my strength and might,
And has become the One who saves me.
This is my God and I will give praise;
The God of my father, and I will grant honor.

Adonai, the Warrior—*Adonai* is God's
name....

The enemy said, "I will pursue and I
will overtake.

I will divide the spoils.

I will have my desire of them.

I will bare my sword—my hand will
overcome them."

You made Your wind blow, the sea
covered them.

They sank like lead in the majestic
waters.

Who is like You, O *Adonai*, among
the gods that are worshiped?

Who is like You, majestic in holiness,
awesome in splendor, working
wonders?...

The last few lines of this reading are in
the siddur. We recite these
lines, the *Mi Chamochah*
מִי־כָמֹכָה, at every evening
and morning worship service
when we remember how
God redeemed us, and we
pray to God to redeem us
now and in the future.

The Death of the Egyptians

A *midrash* teaches that when the
Egyptians began to drown in the sea, the
angels in heaven started singing songs of
praise to God for saving the Israelites.
God turned to the angels and said to
them, "Silence! How can you sing while
my children are drowning?"

We learn from this that God cares
about the death of evildoers, even when
it is necessary to destroy them to save the
innocent. All people are God's children.
As Jews, we feel for the suffering of all
people. We are called upon to show
rachamim רַחֲמִים, mercy and kindness, to
others.

This Sefer Torah *is open to*
Shirat Hayam, *the "Song at
the Sea."* Shirat Hayam *is
presented in a special format
because it is a song.*

The Seder

The *seder* is a ritual meal that we participate in on the first night of Pesach. Many Jews also participate in the *seder* on the second night of Pesach. At the *seder* we tell the story of the Exodus from Egypt. The *seder* ritual helps us relive the Exodus from Egypt every year so that every Jew is able to say, "I myself was a slave in Egypt, and God brought me out of there."

The Order of the Seder

The word *seder* סֵדֶר means "order." We call the Pesach meal a *seder* because we follow a certain order in eating the special foods and reciting the words of the *haggadah* הַגָּדָה, the book that contains the *seder* ritual. The order of the *seder* presented in the *haggadah* has not changed much since ancient times.

A poem that lists the order of the *seder* is printed at the beginning of most *haggadot*. This rhyme is often sung or chanted.

Kadesh, Urechatz קַדֵּשׁ, וּרְחַץ
Blessing over candles and wine
Leader washes hands

Karpas, Yachatz כַּרְפַּס, יַחַץ
Greens dipped into salt water
Break middle *matzah*

Magid, Rachatz מַגִּיד, רָחַץ
Tell the story with second cup of wine
Wash hands

Motzi, Matzah מוֹצִיא, מַצָּה
Blessing over unleavened bread
Eat *matzah*

Maror, Korech מָרוֹר, כּוֹרֵךְ
Bitter herbs
Combination of *matzah* and *maror*

Shulchan Orech שֻׁלְחָן עוֹרֵךְ
Set table—dinner

Tzafun, Barech צָפוּן, בָּרֵךְ
Dessert
Blessing after meal with third cup of wine

Hallel, Nirtzah הַלֵּל, נִרְצָה
Psalms and songs
Conclusion and fourth cup

Identify the Foods of the Seder

The roasted lamb was a sacrifice that the Israelites offered to God on their last night in Egypt. This sacrifice was called the *pesach*. In the days of the Temple, Jews brought their lambs to Jerusalem. They sacrificed their lambs in the Temple and then roasted and ate them outdoors throughout the city.

When the Romans destroyed the Temple in the year 70, Temple sacrifices came to an end. From that time on, Jews roast a shankbone—*zeroa* זְרוֹעַ—and put it on the *seder* table to remember the paschal lamb. The roasted bone reminds us that God passed over the homes of the Jews in Egypt.

The *betzah* בֵּיצָה—roasted egg—is also a reminder of the Temple sacrifices in Jerusalem. Every morning, the priests in the Temple sacrificed one lamb to God on behalf of the entire Jewish people. On festival days, the priests offered a second lamb. The roasted egg reminds us of the second lamb.

Matzah מַצָּה is unleavened bread. One reason we eat *matzah* is to remember the haste in which our people left Egypt. We eat the same food they ate on their journey. We call *matzah* the "bread of affliction," *lechem oni* לֶחֶם עֹנִי. *Matzah* reminds us that we were poor slaves. But *matzah* is also a symbol of our redemption from slavery.

Maror מָרוֹר—bitter herbs—reminds us how bitter it was to live as a slave. To some, *maror* also symbolizes the other periods in history when our people suffered.

We drink four cups of wine to remind us of the four words for redemption in the Torah—God "freed" us, God "saved" us, God "redeemed" us, and God "took" us to be God's own people. The Torah also says that God "brought" us into the Land of Israel. The fifth cup of wine is poured for Elijah the Prophet. It is said that Elijah will announce the coming of the Messianic Age. We place this fifth cup of wine on the *seder* table to express our hope that the days of the Messiah will come soon.

We dip karpas כַּרְפַּס—greens—into salt water and we eat lettuce or *matzah* with *charoset* חֲרֹסֶת. *Karpas* is a sign of spring. The salt water represents the tears of slavery. *Charoset*, a mixture of fruits, nuts, and wine, symbolizes the mortar that the Israelites used to make bricks when they worked for Pharaoh as slaves. In addition, we eat hard-boiled eggs dipped into salt water. Eggs are also a symbol of spring.

Recite the Four Questions

It is customary for a child to recite the Four Questions, which is one of the readings in the *haggadah*. Even if the greatest rabbi in the world were sitting at your *seder* table, a child, not the rabbi, would ask the Four Questions. Traditionally the youngest child recites the Four Questions, but some families

The Sarajevo Haggadah *was created almost 700 years ago in Spain and has been kept in Sarajevo, the capital of Bosnia. In 1992 a civil war broke out in Bosnia and, as a result of the fighting, the* Haggadah *disappeared. During Pesach of 1995, the book reappeared for the first time in years. The president of Bosnia presented the* Haggadah *to the Jewish community of that country. Amid the sounds of jet planes and machine gunfire, the Jews of Sarajevo held a* seder.

שֶׁבְּכָל־הַלֵּילוֹת אָנוּ אוֹכְלִין שְׁאָר
יְרָקוֹת; הַלַּיְלָה הַזֶּה, מָרוֹר.

שֶׁבְּכָל־הַלֵּילוֹת אֵין אָנוּ מַטְבִּילִין
אֲפִלּוּ פַּעַם אֶחָת; הַלַּיְלָה הַזֶּה,
שְׁתֵּי פְעָמִים.

שֶׁבְּכָל־הַלֵּילוֹת אָנוּ אוֹכְלִין בֵּין
יוֹשְׁבִין וּבֵין מְסֻבִּין; הַלַּיְלָה הַזֶּה,
כֻּלָּנוּ מְסֻבִּין.

Why is this night different from all other nights?

On all other nights we eat either leavened bread or matzah; on this night, we eat only matzah.

On all other nights we eat all kinds of herbs; on this night, we especially eat bitter herbs.

On all other nights we do not dip herbs at all; on this night, we dip them twice.

On all other nights we eat in an ordinary manner; on this night, we dine with special ceremony.

A PASSOVER HAGGADAH, CCAR

The Four Questions in the Farissol Haggadah, *which was created in 1515.*

give all the children a chance! It is important for Jewish children to learn the Four Questions well and to be ready for this task.

Here are the Four Questions for you to study:

מַה־נִּשְׁתַּנָּה הַלַּיְלָה הַזֶּה מִכָּל־
הַלֵּילוֹת?

שֶׁבְּכָל־הַלֵּילוֹת אָנוּ אוֹכְלִין חָמֵץ
וּמַצָּה; הַלַּיְלָה הַזֶּה, כֻּלּוֹ מַצָּה.

Cleaning House and Getting Rid of Chametz

All over the world, people do "spring cleaning" when winter ends and warm breezes begin to blow. The whole family gets busy doing chores, getting rid of winter cobwebs, and preparing the house for warm weather. In our family all the sweeping and dusting is done to get rid of any stray crumbs of *chametz* חָמֵץ. This is called *bedikat chametz* בְּדִיקַת חָמֵץ. To prepare for Pesach, we empty out and thoroughly clean our food cabinets and shelves.

When my family and I are almost finished cleaning the house to get rid of all the *chametz*, my father takes little pieces of bread and leaves them hidden in corners. On the night before Pesach, the younger children in the family are given a candle or a flashlight, a feather, and a wooden spoon. The electric lights are turned off. The children use the light to search the house for all the hidden *chametz*. The feather is used to sweep the *chametz* into the wooden spoon.

After the children have found all the hidden *chametz*, we take it outside. Tradition teaches that you burn it in a small fire. Some years we throw the *chametz* into the wind. While burning or throwing the *chametz*, we say the following blessing:

בָּרוּךְ אַתָּה, יְיָ אֱלֹהֵינוּ, מֶלֶךְ הָעוֹלָם, אֲשֶׁר קִדְּשָׁנוּ בְּמִצְוֹתָיו וְצִוָּנוּ עַל בִּעוּר חָמֵץ.

Blessed are You, Adonai our God, Ruler of the universe, who makes us holy with mitzvot and commands us to burn chametz.

After the *chametz* has been cleared from our house, we do not eat *chametz* again until after Pesach.

JUDITH GOLDMAN

The Meaning of Matzah

celebrate here. Next year in the Land of Israel. Now we are all still in bonds. Next year may all be free.

A PASSOVER HAGGADAH, CCAR

When we eat *matzah*, we remember that our ancestors were slaves. The Torah commands us to be kind to strangers "because you were strangers in the land of Egypt." Since we know what it is like to suffer, we do not want anyone else to suffer.

When we sit down to our *seder* meal, we are ready to enjoy the feast. But first we must think of all the poor and oppressed people in the world who are hungry. Our Pesach *seder* inspires us to help feed the hungry and free those who are oppressed. Although we cannot have them all sitting at our *seder* table, our *seder* reminds us that we must try to make the world a better place.

Near the beginning of the *seder*, the part called *Yachatz*, the leader breaks the middle *matzah*. The leader holds up the *matzah* and recites the following:

This is the bread of affliction, the poor bread, which our ancestors ate in the land of Egypt. Let all who are hungry come and eat. Let all who are in need share the hope of Passover. As we celebrate here, we join with our people everywhere. This year we

What Is Chametz?

Chametz is any leavened product that is made from one of five grains. The grains are wheat, rye, oats, barley, and spelt. Spelt is a kind of wheat that grows in the Middle East.

A grain product is leavened if yeast has acted upon it. Yeast is a very small fungus that eats sugar and gives off carbon dioxide, a gas. The action of yeast fills the grain with tiny bubbles, causing it to rise or grow.

Once flour is mixed with water, it becomes *chametz* after eighteen minutes. This is the time it takes for the yeast to begin working. *Matzah* bakers mix flour with water and roll the dough very flat. They put little holes into the dough to prevent it from puffing up and to help it bake quickly; then they put it into the oven. They keep one eye on the clock to make sure that the time from mixing the dough until the baking is complete is not more than eighteen minutes.

Jews have different traditions about eating corn and rice on Pesach. Corn and rice are not among the five grains. Nevertheless, some Jews will not eat these foods on Pesach because they are grains. This is a very important issue in America because so many foods are sweetened with corn syrup. Many Sephardic (Middle Eastern and Spanish) Jews eat corn and rice on Pesach, while many Ashkenazic (European) Jews do not. There is also a question about beans and peas (legumes), including peanuts and peanut butter. If you put beans into water, they will expand. Because of this, some Ashkenazic Jews will not eat beans on Pesach.

A seder tray, a cup of Elijah, and a haggadah *written in Ladino, the language of Sephardic Jews.*

The Omer Period

This box calendar from the 1700s is used to count the Omer. To change the date, one turns a crank in the back of the box each day for forty-nine days.

There are fifty days between Pesach and the holiday of Shavuot. We keep track of these days by "Counting the *Omer*." In Hebrew, this is called *Sefirat Ha'Omer* סְפִירַת הָעֹמֶר. An *omer* is a bundle of grain. In ancient times, Jews would offer a bundle of grain at the Holy Temple on each day between the two holidays. We begin counting the *Omer* at the second *seder*. On the second night of Pesach, we say the blessing for counting the *Omer*:

בָּרוּךְ אַתָּה, יְיָ אֱלֹהֵינוּ, מֶלֶךְ הָעוֹלָם, אֲשֶׁר קִדְּשָׁנוּ בְּמִצְוֹתָיו וְצִוָּנוּ עַל סְפִירַת הָעֹמֶר.

הַיּוֹם יוֹם אֶחָד לָעֹמֶר.

Blessed are You, Adonai our God, Ruler of the universe, who makes us holy with mitzvot and commands us to count the Omer.

Today is the first day of the Omer.

On each night until Shavuot, we announce the day of the *Omer* either at *Ma'ariv*—the evening service—or at the supper table.

Lag Ba'omer

The thirty-third day of the counting of the *Omer* is celebrated as a minor holiday called Lag Ba'omer לַ"ג בָּעֹמֶר. On this day we celebrate the memory of the great rabbis who dedicated their lives to the study of Torah.

After the Romans outlawed the study of Torah in 131 C.E., Rabbi Akiva took his students into the forest. They carried bows and arrows and pretended they were going hunting. Deep in the woods, Rabbi Akiva took a Torah scroll out of a hollow tree and taught his students. When the Romans found them, Rabbi Akiva stood his ground and allowed himself to be arrested while his students

107

escaped. Akiva was executed by the Romans for teaching Torah. In his memory, Jewish elementary school students in Europe used to hold archery contests on Lag Ba'omer. This was a rare day of fun in a long school year.

Sephardic Jews in Israel remember Rabbi Simeon bar Yohai on Lag Ba'omer. According to legend, Rabbi Simeon hid in a cave for twelve years while the Romans searched for him. When the Roman emperor died, Rabbi Simeon came out of the cave and resumed his career as a great rabbi. Tradition says that he wrote the *Zohar*, a holy book that is studied to this day.

In Israel many Jews go to Mount Meron on Lag Ba'omer to visit the grave of Rabbi Simeon bar Yohai. They camp out around big bonfires. They give their three-year-old children their first haircut on this holiday and throw the hair into the fire. Throughout Israel young people celebrate Lag Ba'omer with campfires at which people sing songs, eat, and celebrate late into the night.

In North America many religious schools and youth groups celebrate Lag Ba'omer with field days, on which they hold sporting contests and relay races, enjoy a picnic, and have lots of fun.

SUMMARY

Pesach is one of the *Shalosh Regalim*. It begins in the spring, on the fifteenth of Nisan. Before the holiday starts, many Jews clean their houses to eliminate all traces of *chametz*. During Pesach we eat *matzah* and other unleavened foods. *Matzah* reminds us of the haste with which the Israelites left Egypt during the Exodus.

The *seder* ritual helps us relive the first Pesach in Egypt. The *haggadah*, the book that contains the liturgy for the *seder*, teaches that each one of us must feel as though we ourselves have gone out of Egypt. As part of the *seder* ritual, we eat many symbolic foods, drink four cups of wine, and read the story of the Exodus from Egypt.

In the next chapter we will learn about Yom Hashoah, a day of mourning for the six million Jews who died in the Holocaust.

CHAPTER ELEVEN

YOM HASHOAH

I have taken an oath, to remember it all. To remember, not once to forget!…
An oath: Lest from this we learn nothing.

A. SHLONSKY

Yom Hashoah יוֹם הַשּׁוֹאָה is Holocaust Memorial Day. It is a day of mourning that is observed on the twenty-seventh of Nisan, about a week after the end of Pesach. On Yom Hashoah we remember the six million Jews who were murdered by the Nazis in Europe between the years 1939 and 1945, during World War II.

The Rebellion of the Warsaw Ghetto

Introduction

The Holocaust is the most tragic event in modern Jewish history. Over one-third of the Jews of the world, including 1.5 million children, were put to death by the Nazis.

The events leading to the Holocaust began in 1933 when Adolf Hitler, the leader of the Nazi party, rose to power in Germany. During the next several years, the Nazis enacted many anti-Semitic laws. Jews lost their civic rights. They could not practice professions, attend public schools, or own businesses.

During World War II the Nazis conquered many countries in Europe and enacted anti-Semitic laws in all these countries. By 1938 the Nazis had set up concentration camps for Jews and other prisoners of war. Jews were forced to do hard labor in these camps. Many of them died of exhaustion, disease, and starvation. In 1941 the Nazis began sending Jews to death camps. Six million Jews died in the fifteen concentration and death camps set up by the Nazis.

Some Jews tried to revolt against the Nazi tyranny. The most famous of these revolts was the Warsaw Ghetto Uprising, which lasted from April 19 to May 16, 1943. With few guns and little ammunition, the Jews bravely fought the Nazis until the Germans burned the ghetto to the ground.

This statue in Warsaw, Poland, is a memorial to those who fought in the Warsaw Ghetto Uprising.

The date was *erev* Pesach, April 1943. The place was the Jewish ghetto in Warsaw, Poland. Menachem squinted as he looked out the second-floor window of a deserted building. In his hands he cradled a handmade bomb, a bottle of gasoline with a rag wick. Although Menachem was only fifteen years old, he was already a soldier in the Jewish

Jews in the Warsaw Ghetto being rounded up by German troops.

rebellion against the Nazis.

Menachem waited. He had to wait for many days. The Jews at first succeeded in driving the Germans out of the ghetto. No one had come near Menachem's window. Then the Germans returned in force. They searched the ghetto, building by building.

Menachem liked waiting, and he did not like waiting. Waiting meant that he was still alive. But waiting also reminded him how hungry he was and gave him time to remember. Memories were painful. Menachem remembered how the Nazis had herded him into line one day, along with his parents and his brother and sister. Menachem knew the Germans were lying when they announced that they were taking the Jews to a new work camp where conditions were better.

Menachem had slipped out of the line and had joined those who were hiding and preparing to rebel against the Nazis. Now, as he waited near the window, he wondered if his parents or siblings were still alive.

Suddenly Menachem heard a noise in the street below. He peered out and saw a German command car coming up the street. An important-looking officer sat next to the driver; other officers were in the back seat. "This is the chance I have been waiting for," Menachem said to himself. He lit the fuse, jumped up, and threw the bomb. It splattered on the street and blew up, just behind the German car. He had missed! Menachem stood still for a moment, cursing his bad aim, but when a bullet zinged by his head, he ran for the steps and out of the house through the basement.

Menachem was one of the lucky few who escaped from the Warsaw Ghetto. He hid in the Polish forests until the war ended and then made his way to America. He changed his name to Mike, became a successful businessman, married, and had children. He tried to be happy. But his memories haunted him. One memory especially made him angry—the fact that he had missed his target, that he had thrown away his chance to take revenge on the enemy for the death of his family.

One year, Mike and his family sat around the table at their annual Pesach *seder.* Mike read from the *haggadah:* "In every generation each person should feel as though he or she had gone forth from Egypt."

Mike's daughter, Sarah, suddenly asked him, "Daddy, were you ever a slave?"

Mike had never spoken about his experiences in the Holocaust. No one had ever asked him, not even his wife. But his daughter's question opened up a dam inside him. To his own surprise, Mike found himself telling his daughter all about his Pesach eve in the Warsaw Ghetto, about the sufferings of his family, and about his miraculous survival. He talked for a long time, and when he was finished, he noticed that everyone was looking at him in amazement.

"Wow," said Sarah. "I can't believe my own dad went through all that. You have to come to my school next week and tell all the kids."

Mike agreed. He spoke at his daughter's school, telling his tale of suffering and horror. After that, he spoke to every group of young people that asked him. They wanted to know about the Holocaust, and Mike realized that he needed to tell his story. Sometimes he saw a look of understanding in the eyes of a young student. When that happened, it seemed to Mike as if a bomb were going off, a bomb that this time was hitting its target.

MITZVOT AND MINHAGIM

IT IS A *MITZVAH* TO
- Observe a memorial day for victims of the Holocaust on the twenty-seventh of Nisan.

IT IS A *MINHAG* TO
- Remember the victims of the Holocaust with special services or ceremonies.
- Light six *yahrzeit* candles in memory of the six million Jews who lost their lives in the Holocaust.
- Honor the memory of the *Chasidei Umot Ha'olam,* the Righteous Gentiles, who perished in their attempts to save the lives of Jews during the Holocaust.
- Give *tzedakah* to organizations that preserve the memory of those who died in the Holocaust.

Voices from the Holocaust

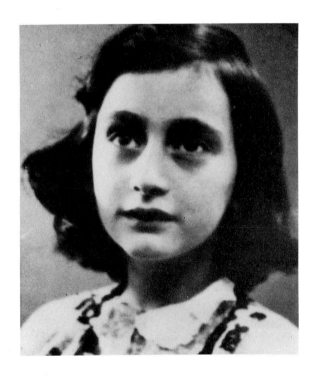

On Yom Hashoah we remember the terrible events of the Holocaust and preserve the memories of the six million Jews who perished. On this day it is customary to read writings by martyrs and survivors of the Holocaust.

The Diary of Anne Frank

Anne Frank, one of the victims of the Holocaust, lived in Amsterdam, Holland, with her family when World War II broke out. In 1940 the Nazis conquered Holland. Shortly thereafter, the Nazis started to restrict Jewish rights. Nazi laws isolated Jews from their Dutch neighbors.

In 1942, when Anne was only thirteen years old, the Nazis started to send Jews to concentration camps. Anne Frank and her family hid in three attic rooms of an office building. For the next two years Anne kept a diary of her thoughts and feelings. In 1944 the Gestapo, the Nazi secret police, discovered the Franks' hiding place. Anne was sent to Bergen-Belson, a death camp in Germany, where she died.

Anne's father, Otto, survived the Holocaust. After the war he returned to Amsterdam and found Anne's diary. *The Diary of Anne Frank* has been translated into more than fifty languages, and millions of people around the world have read her story. In the excerpt below Anne expresses her hopes and fears for the future.

That's the difficulty in these times: ideals, dreams, and cherished hopes rise within us, only to meet the horrible truth and be shattered.

It's really a wonder that I haven't dropped all my ideals, because they seem so absurd and impossible to carry out. Yet I keep them, because in spite of everything, I still believe that people are really good at heart. I simply can't build up my hopes on a foundation consisting of confusion, misery, and death. I see the world gradually being turned into a wilderness; I hear the ever approaching thunder, which will destroy us, too; I can feel the sufferings of millions and yet, if I look up into the heavens, I think that it will all come right, that this cruelty, too, will end, and that peace and tranquillity will return again.

The Last Butterfly

During the Holocaust, Jews were often taken from the cities and towns in which they lived to concentration camps and ghettos far from their homes. Thousands of children were sent to a concentration camp at Terezin in Czechoslovakia. Many of the children were separated from their parents, whom they never saw again. Even though they lived in very harsh and limited conditions, some of these children drew pictures and wrote poetry. These drawings and poems survive to this day. Many of them are published in a book titled *...I never saw another butterfly....* The following was written by Pavel Friedmann, who died in Auschwitz on September 29, 1944.

The last, the very last,
So richly, brightly, dazzlingly yellow.
Perhaps if the sun's tears would sing
 against a white stone ...
Such, such a yellow
Is carried lightly 'way up high.
It went away I'm sure because it
 wished to kiss the world good-bye.
For seven weeks I've lived in here,
Penned up inside this ghetto.
But I have found what I love here.
The dandelions call to me
And the white chestnut candles in
 the court.
Only I never saw another butterfly.
That butterfly was the last one
Butterflies don't live in here,
 in the ghetto.

A painting by a child who was in Terezin, a concentration camp in Czechoslovakia.

I Did Not Speak Out

Martin Niemoller was a Protestant minister in Germany. He spent over eight years in a Nazi concentration camp. After the war he wrote the following in order to remind the world that we cannot afford to keep silent while others are suffering from injustice.

First they came for the Communists
and I did not speak out …
because I was not a Communist.

Then they came for the Socialists
and I did not speak out …
because I was not a Socialist.
Then they came for the trade unionists
and I did not speak out …
because I was not a trade unionist.
Then they came for the Jews
and I did not speak out …
because I was not a Jew.
Then they came for me …
and there was no one left
to speak out for me.

The United States Holocaust Memorial Museum in Washington, D.C.

Yom Hashoah is a recent addition to the Jewish calendar. In 1951 the Knesset, the Israeli Parliament, declared the twenty-seventh of Nisan as Yom Hashoah. They chose this date because they wanted a day that was related to the Warsaw Ghetto Uprising, which began on the eve of Pesach in 1943.

Jews have different ways of observing Yom Hashoah. Since Yom Hashoah was added to the Jewish calendar so recently, there are no specific biblical or rabbinic *mitzvot* associated with this day. Some Jews gather at a synagogue or

Teachers and students at a Yom Hashoah service.

Students at a Jewish day school take turns guarding the six memorial candles and the wall of messages they created for Yom Hashoah.

a Jewish community center for prayers, poems, and special observances. They may light special memorial candles, often six candles to remember the six million murdered Jews. Some Jews join in interfaith ceremonies in which Jews and Christians remember the Holocaust together.

In Israel, in addition to lighting candles and holding special services, Israelis stand at attention for a moment of memory as sirens are sounded throughout the country. It remains to be seen how the observance of Yom Hashoah will develop in the future.

116

The Message of the Holocaust

Young people gather at Auschwitz, the largest concentration camp set up by the Nazis, in Oswiecim, Poland. Each year since 1988, over six thousand students from more than forty countries have converged in Poland on Yom Hashoah to remember the six million Jews who died in the Holocaust.

his work, which teaches people about the Holocaust. Wiesel has said that Jews must never stop teaching the world about the Holocaust. We must make sure, says Wiesel, that such inhumanity is never again allowed to happen to us or to any people. Wiesel has become a defender of victims of hatred all over the world.

The Jewish philosopher Emil Fackenheim is a Holocaust survivor. He also teaches us an important lesson about remembering the Holocaust. According to Jewish tradition, there are 613 *mitzvot* in the Torah. Professor Fackenheim writes that the Holocaust calls on Jews to recognize a new commandment, the 614th *mitzvah*. This *mitzvah*

Why should we remember the Holocaust? What is the message of the Holocaust for all the nations of the world? There is no single answer to this question.

The Holocaust shows us that people are capable of great evil. We cannot simply trust in the goodness of human beings. We must teach people to be good and fight against evil.

Elie Wiesel is a writer who survived Auschwitz. He was awarded the Nobel Peace Prize for

A convention of the Nazi party on September 10, 1935, in Nuremberg, Germany.

forbids Jews to give Hitler a victory after his death.

The 614th *mitzvah* consists of several parts: Jews must do everything they can to survive and grow as a people. Jews must also keep on believing in God so that Judaism does not perish. And Jews must remember the martyrs of the Holocaust so that their memory will not die.

Using the Word Holocaust

The word *Holocaust* has too often been misused. Not every evil on earth is a Holocaust. The destruction of the rain forests or the oppression of one race by another are terrible things, but they are not Holocausts. The Hebrew word for Holocaust, *Shoah* שׁוֹאָה,

means "A great destruction of life, especially by fire." The Holocaust refers to the mass slaughter of European Jewry by the Nazis during World War II.

We honor the memory of our six million martyrs by working to prevent the misuse of the term *Holocaust*.

A Jewish shop in Berlin, with the German word for Jew painted on it by anti-Semitic demonstrators on June 22, 1938.

SUMMARY

Yom Hashoah, Holocaust Memorial Day, is observed on the twenty-seventh of Nisan. The Knesset, Israel's Parliament, created this day in 1951 to honor the memory of the six million Jews who were killed by the Nazis during World War II. On this day we hold special memorial services and light memorial candles.

In the next chapter we will learn about Yom Ha'atzmaut, Israel Independence Day, a modern holiday of celebration.

CHAPTER TWELVE

YOM HA'ATZMAUT

For three things we will offer up our very lives: liberty for Jews to immigrate to our land; the right to rebuild the ruins of our land; and the political independence of the people Israel in our land.

DAVID BEN-GURION

Yom Ha'atzmaut
יוֹם הָעַצְמָאוּת

Israel Independence Day is celebrated on the fifth of Iyar. On this day in 1948, the modern State of Israel proclaimed its independence. When the fifth of Iyar falls on a Friday or Saturday, Yom Ha'atzmaut is celebrated on the Thursday before. In Israel, the day before Yom Ha'atzmaut is Yom Hazikaron יוֹם הַזִּכָּרוֹן—Memorial Day—for those soldiers who fell while defending the State of Israel.

119

If You Will It, It Is Not a Dream

It was January 1895. *The New Free Press*, an Austrian newspaper, sent one of its star reporters, Theodor Herzl, to Paris, France, to cover an important news story. Alfred Dreyfus, a captain in the French army, had been put on trial for spying. Dreyfus was Jewish. Although Dreyfus had proclaimed his innocence, he was found guilty. Many people thought that the captain had been unfairly accused.

Dreyfus on trial before the French military court on August 7, 1899.

The trial brought out the ugly anti-Jewish feelings of many of the citizens of France. After the trial was over, Herzl was sent to report on the public ceremony in which Captain Dreyfus was to be stripped of his rank.

At the time, Herzl was thirty-five years old. Although he was Jewish, he had never paid much attention to his Jewish heritage. What he did do was travel throughout Europe and write articles, stories, and plays. He confided in his diary that he was "a writer of sorts, with little ambition and petty vanities." The events that occurred on the day of the ceremony changed Herzl's life forever.

Herzl watched as Dreyfus was told to step forward. An officer took the sword that hung at Dreyfus's side and broke it in two. Then he tore the epaulets off Dreyfus's uniform. Suddenly the crowd screamed, "Down with the Jews!" Herzl stood in shock. He couldn't believe that he was surrounded by such outright anti-Semitism. Herzl realized then that Europe would never be free of its terrible prejudice against Jews.

When Herzl returned to Vienna, Austria, he started to write down his thoughts about the Dreyfus Affair. Herzl came to the conclusion that the Jews must have a home of their own, a state where they could live in freedom. About a year after the Dreyfus Affair, Herzl wrote a book, *The Jewish State*, in which he outlined his new idea.

Herzl did not know that to the east, in Russia, Jews were already acting on a similar idea. Jews there had formed the Lovers of Zion society, whose goal was to restore the ancient Jewish homeland in Palestine, which was then a province of the Turkish Empire. Some Jews had already gone up to the Land of Israel from Russia.

Theodor Herzl organized an international movement, which he called Zionism. In 1897 he invited Jewish leaders from around the world to the First Zionist Congress in Basle, Switzerland. The Zionists formed an organization, adopted a flag, and started collecting money for their project.

Herzl wrote in his diary: "At Basle, I founded the Jewish state. If I said this aloud today, I would be greeted by laughter. In five years, perhaps, and certainly in fifty years, everyone will see it."

For two thousand years, Jews had prayed to God to send the Messiah to take them back to their land. The Zionists decided not to wait for a miracle but to rebuild the Jewish state on their own. Herzl's plan was to convince the rulers of the most powerful countries to support the creation of the Jewish state. Herzl told the Jewish people, "If you will

Theodor Herzl delivers the opening address to the Second Zionist Congress meeting in Basle, Switzerland, in 1898.

it, it is not a dream"—*Im tirtzu, ain zo agaddah*.

Herzl dedicated his every waking hour to the Zionist dream. He traveled constantly to raise support for a Jewish homeland. But Herzl suffered from a heart ailment. He soon discovered that he did not have the strength to continue his traveling. He caught pneumonia and on July 3, 1904, he died. He was forty-four years old. Only nine years had passed since the Dreyfus Affair had changed the course of his life— and the course of Jewish history.

Although Herzl died, his dream lived on. Fifty-one years after the First Zionist Congress, the Jewish state became a reality. On the night of May 14, 1948, the Jewish leader David Ben-Gurion declared Israel's independence.

On August 14, 1949, Herzl's coffin was taken from a cemetery in Vienna and flown to the new State of Israel. The coffin was brought to a gravesite overlooking the hills of Jerusalem. Thousands of people from all over the land passed by the coffin to pay their respects to the man who had helped make the dream of a Jewish state come true. At the end of the day's ceremonies, the *Mourner's Kaddish* was recited. Theodor Herzl had finally come home.

Herzl's grave, overlooking Jerusalem.

MITZVOT AND MINHAGIM

IT IS A *MITZVAH* TO
- Celebrate the fifth of Iyar as Israel Independence Day, Yom Ha'atzmaut.

IT IS A *MINHAG* TO
- Participate in celebrations in honor of Israel, such as a parade, a fair, a concert, a special service, etc.
- Give *tzedakah* to organizations dedicated to helping the State of Israel.

From the Bible
The Promised Land

Abraham and Lot leave for Canaan.

The first time God speaks to Abraham, God tells him to go to the Land of Israel.

> *Adonai* said to Avram: "Go forth from your native land and from your father's house to the land that I will show you. I will make of you a great nation, and I will bless you."
>
> GENESIS 12:1-2

The Land of Israel is a sign of the covenant between God and the Jews.

> *Adonai* appeared to Abraham's son [Isaac] and said: "Do not go down to Egypt. Stay in the land that I point out to you. Live in this land and I will be with you and bless you; for to you and your descendants I will give all this land, and I shall fulfill My oath that I swore to Abraham, your father. I shall increase your descendants like the stars of heaven, and I shall give them all this land; and all the nations of the earth shall be blessed by you, because Abraham obeyed Me and kept My charge, My commandments, My laws, and My teachings."
>
> GENESIS 26: 2-5

The Babylonians exiled the Jews from the Land of Israel in 586 B.C.E. The Jews swore never to forget their homeland, no matter where they lived.

> By the rivers of Babylon, we sat and wept
> When we remembered Zion....
> If I forget you, O Jerusalem,
> Let my right hand forget her cunning.
> If I do not remember you, let my tongue stick to the roof of my mouth.
> If I do not raise Jerusalem
> Above my highest joy.
>
> PSALMS 137:1, 5-6

123

In the Middle Ages
The Poems of Rabbi
Judah Halevi

the great dangers of the journey. Rabbi Judah Halevi wrote poems about his desire to return to the Land of Israel, including this one, titled "My Heart Is in the East."

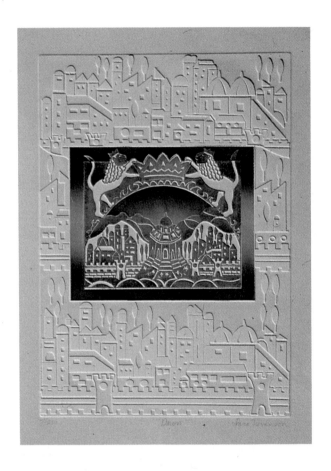

My heart is in the East, and I am in
  the farthest West.
How shall my food have flavor,
  how shall I have any appetite?
How shall I fulfill my vows and
  obligations to God,
While still Zion is a slave to
  Crusaders, and I am in Arab chains?
It would be as light in my eyes to
  leave all the pleasures of Spain,
As it would be dear in my eyes to
  behold the dust of the Temple in
  ruins.

Judah Halevi was born in Spain around the year 1075. He became a leader of the Jews of Spain. He was a rabbi, a doctor, a great teacher of Judaism, and a poet. Rabbi Judah's Hebrew poems are so beautiful that Jews call him "The Sweet Singer of Zion." In his old age, Rabbi Judah visited the Land of Israel, despite

In Modern Times
Hatikvah

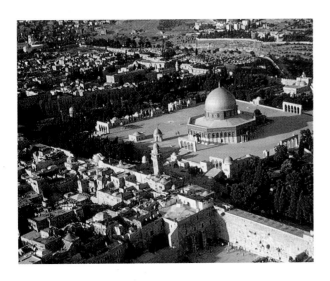

The modern Zionists who founded the State of Israel were inspired by the words of the Bible and by the prayers and poems of every age that express the love of Jews for *Eretz Yisrael*. The Zionists wrote new songs of love for Israel. In 1878, Naftali Imber wrote a Hebrew poem called *Hatikvah* הַתִּקְוָה—"The Hope." Later set to music, it became the anthem of the Zionist movement and then of the State of Israel. The words of the song are:

> As long as in our inner hearts
> A Jewish spirit sings;
> As long as the eye looks to the East,
> Gazing toward Zion.
> Our hope is not lost,
> The hope of two thousand years:

To be a free people in our own land, The Land of Zion and Jerusalem.

YOM YERUSHALAYIM יוֹם יְרוּשָׁלַיִם, JERUSALEM DAY, TAKES PLACE ON THE TWENTY-EIGHTH OF IYAR. ON THIS DAY JEWS CELEBRATE THE LIBERATION OF JERUSALEM. DURING ISRAEL'S WAR OF INDEPENDENCE, JORDAN—AN ARAB COUNTRY THAT BORDERS ISRAEL—CAPTURED THE OLD CITY OF JERUSALEM. UNDER JORDANIAN RULE, JEWS COULD NOT PRAY AT THE WESTERN WALL. DURING THE SIX DAY WAR IN 1967, THE ISRAELI ARMY LIBERATED THE OLD CITY OF JERUSALEM. FOR THE FIRST TIME SINCE THE YEAR 70, THE ENTIRE CITY OF JERUSALEM, INCLUDING THE WESTERN WALL, WAS UNDER JEWISH CONTROL.

Students set up a model of an Israeli market on Yom Yerushalayim.

Yom Ha'atzmaut is another holiday that was recently added to the Jewish calendar. We celebrate Yom Ha'atzmaut on the fifth of Iyar, the day on which David Ben-Gurion declared Israel's independence. Because the fifth of Iyar fell on May 14 in 1948, some communities celebrate Yom Ha'atzmaut on May 14.

Rabbis in Israel and around the world agree that Yom Ha'atzmaut ought to be a holiday for all Jews, but they have not yet decided on the appropriate observances for this new Jewish holiday.

In Israel, Yom Ha'atzmaut is a national patriotic holiday, like the Fourth of July in the United States. There are parades, speeches, parties, and fireworks. Strings of colored lights are hung on all public buildings. Streets are closed off, and people spend the evening of Yom Ha'atzmaut dancing in the streets to music played by live bands on street corners or music played over public-address systems.

In North America, Yom Ha'atzmaut is often celebrated with communal gatherings at synagogues, community centers, and public squares. There may be prayers, readings, and speeches about Israel. Many Jewish communities hold parades, Israeli fairs, or special concerts to celebrate the holiday.

David Ben-Gurion speaks at a ceremony in honor of the tenth anniversary of Israel's independence at the Hebrew University Stadium in Jerusalem.

The day before Yom Ha'atzmaut, Yom Hazikaron—Memorial Day—is observed. Sirens sound throughout Israel at 10:30 A.M. Everyone in the country, whether in a house or on a major highway, stops for two minutes of silence to remember all the people who fought to make Israel a free state and to think about the blessings of the State of Israel.

At 10:30 A.M. the next morning, the sirens sound again for two minutes. This ends Israel's Memorial Day and signals the beginning of Yom Ha'atzmaut. When night falls, the excitement of the holiday begins, with flags, flowers, and celebration.

mountains and waters.

Each guest brought a present that benefited Israel in some way. The party raised a lot of money for *tzedakah*. We also did Israeli dancing and sang Israeli songs. It was great fun to have a birthday party for Israel!

SHARON MORTON

The Israel Day Parade in New York City.

Last year on Yom Ha'atzmaut, I hosted a birthday party for Israel. I served Israeli food. Everybody made big cookies in the shape of the State of Israel and marked the key cities with M&M candies; we used different-colored sprinkles for the

Jewish Devotion to Eretz Yisrael

Jews love and care about Israel for many reasons.

Israel is the ancient Holy Land of the Jewish people. The Jewish tradition teaches that when God created the world, God set aside this piece of land especially for us. Legend has it that Jerusalem, the holiest place on earth, is the center of the universe and the gate to heaven. All the world's prayers rise to God through Jerusalem. Israel is the land of the Bible. In Israel we can visit the actual places in which the events of the Bible and ancient Jewish history took place.

The establishment of the State of Israel is the fulfillment of Jewish hopes and dreams. The rebirth of Israel has ended the centuries during which Jews lived as a people in exile. The State of Israel is a modern democratic country that is a source of pride to Jews everywhere. For many Jews, Israel is an anchor that keeps them from drifting away from their Jewish identity.

Jews all over the world show their support for Israel in many ways. We buy Israeli products. We write letters to our president, senators, and congresspeople and to our local newspapers in support of Israel. We pray for Israel in our synagogues and in our private prayers. We give *tzedakah* for Israel. We go to Israel for a visit or for a longer period to study or work. One of the greatest acts of devotion to Israel is to make *aliyah* עֲלִיָּה, "to go up" to live in Israel.

Youth aliyah *from Europe on a ship headed for Israel.*

The United Nations Votes to Partition Palestine

David Ben-Gurion signs Israel's Declaration of Independence.

November 29, 1947. Jews throughout the world sat by their radios, waiting for news. On that day the United Nations was going to vote on the partition of Palestine. If the UN voted to divide Palestine between the Jews and Arabs, the Jewish state would become a reality!

The British had taken control of the land of Palestine from the Turks in 1917, during World War I. In the famous Balfour Declaration of that year, the British had promised that the Jews could

establish a homeland in Palestine. But the British had also made promises to the Arabs. As a result of these conflicting promises, both the Arabs and the Jews claimed the land of Palestine.

In 1947 the British asked the United Nations to decide what should be done with Palestine. At that time, over 500,000 Jews lived in the Land of Israel. The UN recommended dividing the land into a Jewish state and an Arab state. The Jews agreed to this proposal. The Arabs were against it. They wanted only an Arab state. The Arab nations and their allies were prepared to vote against the partition plan.

The Jews waited and wondered: Would the nations of the world accept the Jewish claim to the Land of Israel? The Jews of Europe had just lost six million of their people in the Holocaust. Hundreds of thousands of homeless Jews were living in tent camps all over Europe, waiting for the answer to that question.

The United States did not decide until October 1947 whether it would favor or oppose the plan. Once President Truman decided in favor of a Jewish state, he urged other nations to vote for the partition of Palestine. The partition plan needed a two-thirds majority in the United Nations to win. The roll call of nations was alphabetical. The two most

Nations had voted to create a Jewish state!

Jews everywhere danced and sang with joy. In Tel Aviv, Jerusalem, and New York, the streets filled with Jewish revelers. The sound of the *shofar* announced the great news. In six months the British would leave, and the Jews would have their own state! Although the Arab nations had announced that they would invade the new state on the day the British left, no one seemed concerned. It was a day to rejoice!

powerful nations, the United States and the Soviet Union, both voted in favor of a Jewish state. Jews around the world held their breath as the votes were announced. The final vote was thirty-three nations in favor, thirteen against, with the rest not voting. The United

SUMMARY

Yom Ha'atzmaut became a holiday after Israel won its War of Independence in 1949. We usually celebrate Yom Ha'atzmaut on the fifth of Iyar, which is the day Israel declared its independence.

Because Yom Ha'atzmaut is such a new holiday, no "official" way of celebrating it has been established.

Picnics, parades, concerts, and fireworks are all part of the celebration. Some communities hold more formal, solemn observances that may include prayers, readings, and speeches. Yom Ha'atzmaut is a special day on which we celebrate Israel's importance and many accomplishments.

CHAPTER THIRTEEN

SHAVUOT

*Shout joyfully to **Adonai**, all the earth! Serve the Eternal with gladness.*
Come before God's presence with singing.

PSALMS 100: 1-2

Shavuot

שָׁבוּעוֹת

is celebrated on the sixth day of Sivan, in late spring. Shavuot, the third of the *Shalosh Regalim*, is called *Zeman Matan Toratenu* זְמַן מַתַּן תּוֹרָתֵנוּ—the "Time of the Giving of Our Torah." On this holiday we praise God for the gift of revelation. Shavuot is also *Chag Habikurim* חַג הַבִּכּוּרִים—the "Festival of the First Fruits." We thank God for the end of the grain harvest in the Land of Israel and for the harvest of the first ripe summer fruits.

Israel at Mount Sinai

Before God created the universe, God first wrote the Torah. Then God looked into the Torah and created the universe, just like a builder who follows a plan when designing a house.

When the time came for God to give the Torah to humankind, God began searching for a nation that would be willing to receive God's gift. God went to one powerful nation and said to its people, "Will you accept My Torah?"

"What is written in it?" they asked.

"You shall not murder," God said. "You shall not steal."

"We cannot accept the Torah," replied this nation. "We live by conquering other countries, robbing their people, and killing them."

God went to another nation, one that was wealthy, and asked its people to accept the Torah.

"What is written in it?" they asked.

"You shall have just weights and measures," God said. "You shall not put a stumbling block before the blind."

"We cannot accept the Torah," replied the people of this nation, "because we would not make enough money if we could not cheat and deceive."

God went from nation to nation, asking the people whether they would accept the Torah, but each nation refused after they heard what was in it. Finally God came to the smallest and weakest nation on earth, the Children of Israel. God

In this illustration from the Rothschild Machzor, *created in Florence in 1492, Moses receives the Ten Commandments on Mount Sinai.*

delivered them from slavery in Egypt, took them to Mount Sinai, and asked them, "Will you accept My Torah?"

"We will do and we will hear all that *Adonai* has spoken," replied the Israelites as one.

At that moment, God sent angels to place a crown on the head of every Israelite present because all of them had agreed to observe God's commandments even before they heard what those commandments were. God said to Israel, "If you obey Me and keep My covenant, you shall be My special people. All the earth is Mine, but you shall be a nation of priests, a holy nation."

It is said that all the mountains in the world argued over which one would be chosen as the place where God would give the Torah. One mountain proclaimed, "I am the most beautiful." Another boasted, "I am the tallest mountain." To them God said, "Neither you nor you but Mount Sinai, which is a humble and ordinary mountain, shall be the site." So, too, God chose the Israelites to receive the Torah.

MITZVOT AND MINHAGIM

IT IS A *MITZVAH* TO

- Observe Shavuot as a festival day on the sixth day of Sivan, the fiftieth day after Pesach.
- Reaffirm the *berit* בְּרִית, the covenant between God and the Jewish people. We do this when we hear the reading of the Ten Commandments at services and promise to fulfill our responsibilities as an *Am Berit* עַם בְּרִית, a "Covenant People."
- Read the Book of Ruth מְגִלַּת רוּת, one of the five *megillot*.

IT IS A *MINHAG* TO

- Stay awake late into the night on Shavuot, studying the Torah. This *minhag* is called *Tikun Leil Shavuot* תִּקּוּן לֵיל שָׁבוּעוֹת.
- Eat fruits and dairy foods. The fruits remind us that Shavuot is the Festival of the First Fruits. Dairy is a symbol for the Torah, which is sweet and provides us with sustenance.
- Decorate our home and the temple with greenery and fresh flowers.

Tikun Leil Shavuot

Jews believe that God's message is revealed to us in two important books, the Bible and the Talmud. The Bible, or *Tanach* תַּ"נָךְ, consists of twenty-four books. The first five books are the Torah. The remaining nineteen books make up the two other sections of the *Tanach*, the Prophets נְבִיאִים and the Writings כְּתוּבִים. The Talmud contains the laws and traditions of the ancient rabbis. The Talmud, which is divided into six sections, tells us how to live by the Torah.

Together, the twenty-four books of the *Tanach* and the six sections of the Talmud make up what Jews call "the whole Torah."

Around the year 1530, in the city of Safed in the Land of Israel, a group of rabbis began the custom of studying "the whole Torah" in one night on Shavuot. How could they study all this material in one night? They read a small portion from each of the fifty-four *parashiyot* of the Torah, a small selection from each of the other nineteen books of the *Tanach*, and readings from each of the sixty-three tractates of the Talmud.

The Ten Commandments are introduced in the following way: "And God spoke these words...."

We, too, can study "the whole Torah" in one class session. In the mini-*tikun* below, we will study a verse from each book of the Torah. Then we will study a verse from the Prophets and a verse from the Writings, the two other sections of the *Tanach*. Finally we will study one portion from each of the six sections of the Talmud.

Tanach

GENESIS *Adonai* said to Avram: "Go forth from your native land and from your father's house to the land that I will show you. I will make of you a great nation, and I will bless you; I will make your name great, and you shall be a blessing." 12:1-2

EXODUS God spoke to Moses and said to him, "I am *Adonai*. I appeared to Abraham, Isaac, and Jacob as *El Shaddai*, but I did not make Myself known to them by My name יְהֹוָה. 6:2-3

LEVITICUS You shall be holy, for I, *Adonai* your God, am holy…. Love your neighbor as yourself: I am *Adonai*. 19:2, 18

NUMBERS They marched from the mountain of *Adonai*, a distance of three days. The Ark of the Covenant of *Adonai* traveled in front of them on that three days' journey to seek out a resting place

for them; and *Adonai*'s cloud kept above them by day, as they moved on from camp. 10:33-34

DEUTERONOMY Hear, O Israel, *Adonai* is our God, *Adonai* is One. You shall love *Adonai* your God with all your heart and with all your soul and with all your might. 6:4-5

PROPHETS God has told you: "O mortal, what is good and what does *Adonai* require of you: Only to do justice and to love mercy and to walk humbly with your God." MICAH 6:8

WRITINGS *Adonai* is gracious and compassionate, slow to anger and abounding in kindness. *Adonai* is good to all, and God's mercy is upon all God's works. PSALMS 145:9-10

Talmud

ZERAIM If one sees shooting stars, earthquakes, lightning, thunder, and storms, one says: "Blessed is the One whose power and might fill the world." If one sees mountains, hills, seas, rivers, and deserts, one says: "Blessed is the Source of Creation…. For rain and for good news, one says: "Blessed is the One who is good and does good." For bad news, one says: "Blessed is *Adonai*, the true Judge." BERACHOT 9:2

MOED Four times in the year the world is judged: on Pesach, for grain; on Shavuot, for the fruits of the tree; on Rosh Hashanah, all that came into the world pass before God like flocks of sheep; and on Sukot, all are judged for water. *ROSH HASHANAH 1: 2*

NASHIM The sages have said: "There are four kinds of vows that a person is not required to fulfill—vows made in excitement, vows of exaggeration, vows made in error, and vows in which circumstances prevent [the person from fulfilling the vow]." *NEDARIM 3:1*

NEZIKIN If two people each lay hands upon a piece of cloth and they both say, "I found it!" or they both say, "All of it is mine!" they must each make an oath [in court] that at least half of it belongs to him. Then they divide the cloth between them. *BABA METZIA 1:1*

KODASHIM [A priest] who desired [the honor of] cleaning the ashes from the altar rose up early and immersed himself in the *mikveh* [the ritual bath of purification] before the coming of the officer [in charge of the priests]. At what time did the officer come? Sometimes at cockcrow, sometimes a little sooner or later. The officer came and knocked on the door of the place where the priests were gathered, and they opened the door for him. He said, "Let those who have immersed themselves choose lots!" They chose lots, and whoever the lot fell upon was chosen. *TAMID 1:2*

TOHOROT Judah, an Ammonite who had converted to Judaism, came before the Sanhedrin [the High Court]. He asked them, "May I be counted as a Jew?" Rabban Gamliel said, "You are forbidden." Rabbi Joshua said, "You are permitted." Rabban Gamliel said to Judah, "The Torah says, 'An Ammonite or a Moabite shall not be admitted into the congregation of *Adonai*.'" (Deuteronomy 23:4) Rabbi Joshua said to Gamliel, "Yes, but are the Ammonites and Moabites of today the same people? Long ago, King Sennacherib of Assyria came and mixed up all of the nations…." And [the majority voted] to permit Judah to join the Jewish people. *YADAIM 4:4*

The Ten Commandments

There are 613 *mitzvot* in the Torah. The Torah calls one group of *mitzvot Aseret Hadibrot* עֲשֶׂרֶת הַדִּבְּרוֹת—the Ten Commandments. These *mitzvot* differ from the others because, according to the Torah, they were spoken by God directly to the entire Jewish people as they stood at the foot of Mount Sinai. These ten *mitzvot* are also accepted by Christians. Jews and Christians alike recognize the Ten Commandments as the basic laws of our society. The Torah portion for Shavuot contains the Ten Commandments.

1. **I AM *ADONAI* YOUR GOD, WHO TOOK YOU OUT OF THE LAND OF EGYPT.**

2. **YOU SHALL HAVE NO OTHER GODS BESIDE ME. YOU SHALL NOT MAKE IDOLS OF ANYTHING IN THE SKY, ON THE LAND, OR IN THE WATER. YOU SHALL NOT BOW DOWN TO THEM OR SERVE THEM.**

3. **YOU SHALL NOT SWEAR FALSELY BY THE NAME OF GOD.**

4. **REMEMBER THE SABBATH AND KEEP IT HOLY.**

5. **HONOR YOUR FATHER AND YOUR MOTHER.**

6. **YOU SHALL NOT MURDER.**

7. **YOU SHALL NOT COMMIT ADULTERY.**

8. **YOU SHALL NOT STEAL.**

9. **YOU SHALL NOT TESTIFY FALSELY UNDER OATH.**

10. **YOU SHALL NOT COVET.**

EXODUS 20

Confirmation

Teenagers at their confirmation ceremony, 1916.

For thousands of years, Jews have had our own school system. Every Jewish boy went to school six days a week, starting when he was about the age of five. Until modern times, girls were not sent to school regularly, but many of them were taught to read and write at home. Nearly every Jew read the entire Bible and knew many of the laws and rules of Judaism. Every Jewish community had a *bet midrash* בֵּית־מִדְרָשׁ—a house of study—where men went to study together.

About a hundred or more years ago, many countries established public schools for all children. As Jews began attending the public schools instead of the Jewish schools, the hours they devoted to Jewish learning decreased to just a few hours a week. In Germany, the first modern country in which Jews went to public schools, many Jewish boys ended their Jewish education right after their bar mitzvah בַּר מִצְוָה, at age thirteen, before they knew much about Judaism.

The leaders of Reform Judaism realized that Judaism would grow only if Jewish boys and girls received a good Jewish education. These leaders eliminated the bar mitzvah ceremony and replaced it with the confirmation ceremony, which occurs when a Jewish child reaches the age of fifteen or sixteen. In this way, Jewish children would continue to receive a formal Jewish education for a few more years. In contrast to the bar mitzvah, from which girls were excluded, confirmation was for both boys and girls.

Soon all the Reform congregations in Germany and America began this observance. Today students in most Reform temples, as well as in many Conservative congregations, prepare to become bar or bat mitzvah and then also prepare for confirmation, which has become the next level of achievement in Jewish education.

Shavuot is a good time to hold confirmation. This festival occurs at the end of the school year. More important, Shavuot is the Season of the Giving of Our Torah. It reminds us that at the beginning of our history, the Jewish people promised God that we would accept the Torah, learn it, and live by it. Each confirmation student is asked to imagine that he or she is standing at the foot of Mount Sinai, prepared to repeat the promise of our ancestors: "We will do and we will hear [all that *Adonai* has spoken]."

Although confirmation ceremonies may vary from one congregation to the next, most of them include the following:

- A procession of confirmands who carry flowers or food baskets, which resembles the Shavuot processions in the ancient Temple.
- A creative presentation of a Jewish theme by the confirmands.
- Participation in Shavuot services, including the reading of the Ten Commandments from the Torah.
- A pledge by the confirmands to live by the Torah.

JEWISH FAMILY ALBUM

When I was growing up, Shavuot was always linked to confirmation and the idea of the giving of the Torah. We attended services as a family and participated in the confirmation cantata, which was written by the class.

The year of my confirmation, the sanctuary lights were dimmed and the confirmands carried lit candles. I remember feeling a sense of overwhelming responsibility about confirming my beliefs as a Jewish adult as we repeated the words of our ancestors: *Na'aseh venishma*—"We will do and we will hear."

Now that I am a rabbi, I often recall

the candles that illuminated my confirmation service. The memory of their glowing lights inspires me to teach Torah to my own students.

RABBI JOAN GLAZER FARBER

What Did God Say at Mount Sinai?

What exactly did the Jews hear as the Word of God at Mount Sinai? What was written on the two tablets that Moses brought down from the mountain?

It may have been the Ten Commandments written on the two tablets. It may have been a larger group of laws. Some Jews believe that the entire Five Books of the Torah were written on the tablets. This is known as the Written Law. Judaism also teaches that while Moses was on the mountain, he learned from God all the laws and rules that would someday be written down in the Talmud. This is known as the Oral Law.

The study of history shows us that it is very unlikely that Moses brought down from Sinai the whole Torah as we have it now. Liberal Jews believe that the words Moses brought down on the tablets were the beginning of what over many centuries became the Torah. There is no way to know exactly what was written on the tablets and no way to know which Jewish traditions go all the way back to the time of Moses.

It is difficult for us to imagine what the Israelites heard at Mount Sinai. One tradition says that each Jew heard a different message, and afterward no two Jews could agree on exactly what they had heard. Each Jew heard the message that he or she was prepared and able to hear from God.

Jews hold different ideas about what God said to Moses and all the Jews at Mount Sinai. But most Jews agree on the following: God and the Jewish people met at Mount Sinai. On that day, the Jewish people entered into a covenant with God. It is a covenant that will last for all time.

The Story of Ruth

On the festival of Shavuot, we read the story of Ruth, which takes place during the grain harvest in ancient Israel.

Once there was a man from the tribe of Judah named Elimelech, who lived in Bethlehem. Because there was a drought in the country of Judah, Elimelech took his wife Naomi and his two sons and went to live in the land of Moab. The two sons took wives from among the Moabite women. Elimelech and his two sons died in Moab.

When Naomi decided to return home to Bethlehem, her two daughters-in-law wanted to go with her.

Naomi said to them, "My daughters, return to your families and marry from among your own people."

One of the women listened to Naomi and returned to her home. The other daughter-in-law, Ruth, said to Naomi, "Do not beg me to leave you or to stop following you, for wherever you go, I shall go, and wherever you stay, I shall stay. Your people shall be my people, and your God, my God. Where you die, will I die, and there will I be buried. Thus and more may *Adonai* do to me if anything but death parts you and me." And so Ruth went back to Bethlehem with Naomi. They arrived at the beginning of the barley harvest.

The next day, Ruth went out to glean in the fields—that is, to pick up the stalks of grain that the reapers dropped, for these were left for the poor. By luck, Ruth went to glean in the fields belonging to Boaz, a relative of Naomi. It was a law in ancient Israel that if a man died childless, as Ruth's late husband had, his widow was obligated to marry one of his relatives and name the first child after the deceased.

When Boaz saw Ruth gleaning in his fields, he ordered his reapers to leave extra stalks of grain for her, so that she could collect an added portion. At midday, when all the reapers sat down to eat, Boaz invited Ruth to enjoy the shade of the harvest booth and gave her some food.

Ruth went home to her mother-in-law, Naomi, that night with a full bundle of grain. Naomi was happy when she heard that Ruth had been gleaning in the fields of her relative Boaz, for she knew that he was a good and kind person. Naomi said to Ruth, "Do not go to anyone else's fields, but go every day to Boaz's fields." Ruth obeyed Naomi, and she gleaned beside Boaz's reaper girls every day during the barley harvest and the wheat harvest.

When the harvest came to an end, Naomi said to Ruth, "It is time to think about the future. Tonight Boaz will be with the other men, winnowing barley on the threshing floor. Bathe and dress and go to him there, but wait until he has eaten and drunk before you make yourself known to him. He will tell you what to do."

Ruth did as Naomi told her. When Boaz saw Ruth, he said, "May God bless you for choosing me above all other men." But Boaz then told Ruth that there was another man who was a closer relative to her late husband than he was. Only if that man agreed could he, Boaz, marry Ruth. Then Boaz gave Ruth some grain to take back to Naomi as a gift.

The next day, Boaz went up to the city gate of Bethlehem and waited there for the relative about whom he had spoken. When the man appeared, Boaz talked to him about Ruth, and the man agreed before ten of the elders of the city that he would give up his right to marry Ruth in favor of Boaz.

And so Boaz and Ruth were married. Their son was named Obed. He became the father of Jesse, who was the father of David. David became king of Israel.

ADAPTED FROM THE SCROLL OF RUTH

SUMMARY

On Shavuot we commemorate the giving of the Torah at Mount Sinai. Shavuot is also called the Festival of the First Fruits because it marks the end of the harvest in Israel. Many congregations celebrate confirmation on Shavuot. The Book of Ruth, one of the five *megillot*, is read on Shavuot.

In the next chapter we will learn about the final holy day of the Jewish year, Tishah Be'av.

CHAPTER FOURTEEN

TISHAH BE'AV

By the rivers of Babylon, we sat and wept when we remembered Zion.

PSALMS 137:1

Tishah Be'av
תִּשְׁעָה בְּאָב
is a day of mourning and fasting that falls in mid-summer, on the ninth day of Av. Many of the saddest events in Jewish history occurred on this date: the destruction of the First Temple in 586 B.C.E.; the destruction of the Second Temple in 70 C.E.; the expulsion of the Jews from England in 1290; and the expulsion of the Jews from Spain in 1492. Tishah Be'av is a solemn day on which we remember these events in Jewish history.

143

The Babylonians Destroy the First Temple—586 B.C.E.

King Nebuchadnezzar ruled over the powerful Babylonian Empire. Nebuchadnezzar's armies conquered one country after another, including the kingdom of Judah. They surrounded the city of Jerusalem and conquered it. On the Ninth of Av, the Babylonians set fire to the city and the Temple that King Solomon had built. They tore down the walls of the city of Jerusalem. They killed many Jews and exiled most of the others to Babylon.

About fifty years after the destruction of Jerusalem, King Cyrus the Great of Persia conquered Babylon. King Cyrus gave the Jews permission to return home and rebuild Jerusalem. The Jews built a new Temple and rejoiced that their exile had come to an end.

Four great empires rose one after the other. The Persians conquered the

This tapestry, created in the sixteenth century, depicts a battle between the Romans, led by Vespasian, and the Jews. In 70 C.E., on the Ninth of Av, the Romans destroyed the Second Temple.

Babylonians. The Greeks conquered the Persians. The Romans conquered the Greeks. The Roman Empire was the mightiest empire the world had ever known.

The Romans ruled with great cruelty. They tried to destroy the Jewish way of life. In the year 66 C.E., the Jews rebelled and forced the Romans to leave Judah. But the Romans came back the next year with three large armies. They conquered the countryside and then surrounded Jerusalem. The city held out for two years.

Just as the Romans surrounding the city of Jerusalem were about to break through, the great scholar Rabbi Yohanan ben Zakkai called on the generals in charge of the Jewish rebellion to surrender the city. But the Jewish generals refused. Rabbi Yohanan tried to save at least some Jews on his own. He started a rumor that he had died. Then he had his followers carry him out of the city in a white shroud. Once he was past the guards, Rabbi Yohanan threw aside his shroud and went before Vespasian, the Roman general, to surrender. "Hail, O emperor!" said Yohanan.

"I am not the emperor, only a general," replied Vespasian.

At that moment, a messenger burst into

Vespasian's tent with the news from Rome that Vespasian had just been elected the new Roman emperor.

"Since you were the first to greet me as emperor, I will grant you a wish. What is your request?" asked Vespasian.

"All I ask of you," replied Rabbi Yohanan, "is that you spare the lives of the Torah sages. Let me begin a Jewish school in the city of Yavneh." Vespasian granted this request.

In the summer of the year 70, the Romans finally took Jerusalem. In their rage they killed many people and destroyed every home and building in the city.

The Second Temple, the center of Jewish life, had stood for nearly five hundred years. The Jews had rebuilt it into one of the most beautiful buildings in the ancient world. The Romans waited a few days. On the Ninth of Av, the very day of the destruction of the First Temple, the Romans burned down the Second Temple. They knocked down all the stones of the Temple so that only the outer Western Wall of the Temple courtyard remained standing.

It was a tragic time for the Jews. But Rabbi Yohanan ben Zakkai gathered all the wise sages in Yavneh. The sages became the leaders and teachers of the Jewish people. They saved Judaism in its darkest hour.

MITZVOT AND MINHAGIM

IT IS A *MITZVAH* TO
- Fast on Tishah Be'av, beginning at sunset.
- Read or chant *Eichah*, the Book of Lamentations, after the evening service.
- Postpone the observance of Tishah Be'av until Sunday if the Ninth of Av falls on Shabbat because we may not fast or mourn publicly on Shabbat except if Yom Kippur falls on Shabbat.

IT IS A *MINHAG* TO
- Eat foods typically eaten by those in mourning, such as eggs, lentils, and chick-peas, before beginning the fast.
- Maintain the mood of Tishah Be'av by keeping the meal we eat before the fast modest and simple and by going about our usual activities in a somber mood.

Lamentations

The prophet Jeremiah laments the destruction of Jerusalem.

The Book of Lamentations, *Eichah* אֵיכָה, is one of the five *megillot* in the Bible. It expresses sorrow about the destruction of Jerusalem by the Babylonians. The prophet Jeremiah lived during those horrible times. Jewish tradition says that the prophet Jeremiah wrote the Book of Lamentations.

Alas, how alone sits the city that once was full of people! She has become like a widow. She was once great among the nations, famous in many lands, but now she is enslaved. 1:1

All her people sigh as they beg for bread. They trade their treasures for a bit of food to keep alive. Look, O God, and see how I have become desperate! 1:11

For these things I weep: My eye, my eye runs down with water, because the Comforter that should relieve my soul is far from me. My children are alone, because the enemy has won. Zion spreads out her hands, and there is no one to comfort her. 1:16-17

God has despised the altar, rejected the Holy Place. God has handed over the walls of the palaces to the enemy. They shout in the Temple as if it were a festival day. 2:7

You, *Adonai*, will reign forever, from generation to generation. Will You forget us forever, abandon us for days on end? Return us to You, O *Adonai*, and we shall return to You. Make us new, as in days of old! 5:19-21

Before and after Tishah Be'av

The *haftarot* from early summer until Rosh Hashanah in the fall reflect the theme of Tishah Be'av.

On the three Sabbaths before Tishah Be'av, we read the *haftarot* of rebuke. A rebuke is a warning that we will be punished if we do not change our ways.

On the seven Sabbaths after Tishah Be'av, we read the *haftarot* of consolation. Consolation is the act of comforting someone who is sad. In these *haftarot* the prophets promise the Jews that God will forgive us, take us back in love, and give us a greater glory than we had before.

The final *haftarah* of rebuke is from the Book of Isaiah. It includes the following:

> Hear, O heavens, and give ear, O earth, for *Adonai* has spoken: "I have brought up children, but they have turned against Me. An ox knows its master and a donkey knows the stall of its owner. Why doesn't Israel know? Why don't My people think about this?... Wash yourselves clean! Remove your evil deeds from My sight and stop doing wrong! Learn to do good, seek justice, take care of the oppressed. Look after the orphan and the widow!... Zion will be saved through justice and her exiles through righteousness." 1:2-3; 16-17; 27

The first *haftarah* of consolation begins:

> "Take comfort, take comfort, My people," says your God. "Speak kindly to Jerusalem and call to her that she has finished her term, completed her punishment, for she has received from God double for all her sins."... Look! *Adonai* our God is coming in strength to rule with power. See, God is bringing a reward and a payment. Like a shepherd, God pastures the flock, gathering the lambs in the arms of the Holy One and holding them tight, gently leading the mother sheep. 40:1-2; 10-11

Tishah Be'av through the Ages

A view of the Temple Mount and holy sites in Jerusalem.

Although the observance of Tishah Be'av is not commanded in the Torah, during the almost two thousand years of the Second Exile, Jews have observed the Ninth of Av as a day of fasting and sorrow. They prayed for an end to the exile. Jews believed that God had exiled them from the Land of Israel because they had sinned. They prayed for forgiveness and asked God to send the Messiah—a leader who would defeat their enemies, take the Jews back to the Land of Israel, and rebuild the Temple.

With the rise of Reform Judaism in the early 1800s, Reform Jews began to question whether they should continue to observe Tishah Be'av. At that time, countries in Europe began granting citizenship to Jews. As a result, many Jews living in Europe no longer felt as though they were living in exile. They believed that human progress would lead to a Messianic Age, when there would be plenty of everything for everyone, hatred and war would cease, and Jews would live happily among their neighbors in every country.

More recently, Jews have questioned whether we should observe a fast day in memory of the destruction of Jerusalem now that the State of Israel has been established and the city of Jerusalem is flourishing as Israel's capital.

Nonetheless, many Jews continue to observe Tishah Be'av. We have discovered that progress can create evil as well as good, nuclear weapons as well as abundant crops. There is still much hatred, war, and sorrow in the world. Although Jews may not be in exile any longer, we recognize that the world is in need of repair and healing. On Tishah Be'av we learn about Jewish history and explore our role in shaping the Jewish future. On this day we express our hope for the coming of the Messianic Age.

A mizrach, *like the one pictured here, is often placed on the eastern wall of a Jewish home to indicate the direction toward Jerusalem, which Jews always face when they pray. This* mizrach *depicts the celebration of Jewish holidays.*

SUMMARY

Tishah Be'av is a fast day that is observed on the ninth day of the month of Av. It commemorates the destruction of the First and Second Temples in Jerusalem. Because many other Jewish tragedies also occurred on or near Tishah Be'av, it has become a day for mourning and remembering many of the tragic events in Jewish history. On Tishah Be'av, Jews fast and read the Book of Lamentations, one of the five *megillot*. It is a day for thinking about the past and the future of the Jewish people and looking forward to the dawn of the Messianic Age.

INDEX

153